SPLIT-SECOND COURAGE

What If Your Fears
Were the Key to Your Dreams?

SPLIT-SECOND COURAGE

CHRISTINE M. CONTI

Niche Pressworks

SPLIT-SECOND COURAGE

ISBN-13: 978-1-952654-41-1 Hardback

978-1-952654-39-8 Paperback

978-1-952654-40-4 eBook

Photographs by Lifetime Impressions Photography; http://lifetimeimpressionsphotography.com

Published by Niche Pressworks; http://NichePressworks.com

Indianapolis, IN

DEDICATION

To Michael

"The Best Is Yet to Come"

Contents

Foreword

Perhaps the biggest misconception we have of courageous people is that we think they're *never* afraid. We tend to see them as superhumans with extraordinary powers, and we marvel at their ability to take risks and overcome seemingly impossible odds.

One could easily get that same impression of Christine Conti, and with good reason. We watch her crush Boston Marathons, tackle triathlons, and run insane one-hundred-mile races. The fact that she does all of this with rheumatoid arthritis (RA) only adds to her legendary status.

But Christine will be the first one to tell you that she, too, feels fear. She experiences self-doubt just like the rest of us. Thus, in most ways, she's no different from you or me. The difference, however, is that Christine is able to conquer that fear, and she does so using Split-Second Courage.

I've been blessed to spend my entire professional career surrounded by courageous people like Christine—first, as a career army officer with combat deployments to Iraq and Afghanistan, and later, as a faculty member at West Point and now at Seton Hall University, where I get to develop the next generation of courageous leaders.

I've learned so much from being around courageous people. I'm most fascinated with understanding how they overcome the same fears and anxieties that tend to hold others back, myself included. How do they do it?

One of the best definitions of courage I've heard comes from the US Army's 82nd Airborne. True courage, they said, is when you're afraid, but you go anyway.

I've thought about that definition a lot throughout my professional career. I thought about it as an attack helicopter pilot flying combat missions in the Afghan night. I thought about it as the cameras went live just before I testified in front of Congress. I thought about it when I became a dad for the first time. And I thought about it when I decided to start my own business coaching athletes and business leaders on the mental game.

In each of these moments, I was most definitely afraid, but I was able to muster the courage to overcome my fears and "go anyway."

Some may chalk this behavior up as a trait that one is simply born with, but I disagree. I believe that Split-Second Courage can be learned like any other skill. I think we can teach others how to cross that chasm of self-doubt and go after what they want so they can live their best lives.

And with *Split-Second Courage*, Christine Conti does just that. She knows how to tap into Split-Second Courage because she's done it herself, and she passes along that wisdom now to you. My hope is that you'll do the same and pass this book, and the wisdom in it, on to those you care about.

Bryan C. Price, PhD
Lieutenant Colonel (USA Retired)
Founder, Top Mental Game

Preface: 'Let's Roll'

IT TAKES A SPLIT SECOND to make a decision, but for some people, all the time in the world is still not enough to muster up the courage to act. Are you one of them? If so, what's the cost of your hesitation?

Think about it: The more you dare to act, the more you dare to achieve. Over decades of personal experience and the hundreds of interviews I have conducted with highly successful and fascinating people from around the globe, I have learned valuable secrets that can help you to unlock your greatest potential. You can learn to seize the courage to act in the moment when you need to or take "unexpected" actions in general situations because you know they're right.

As you read this book, think about the things you desire to have or do and how they would change your life. How would they improve your relationships, health, finances, and happiness? If they would be so wonderful, why aren't you doing anything to get them? The time is now to grow your Split-Second Courage!

Whenever I fly, I can't help but think back to the catastrophic events that took place on that beautiful clear day on September 11, 2001. Though a native New Yorker, I was far from the city that day. So, I watched with millions of others via TV broadcast as the second plane disappeared into the massive steel and concrete siding of Tower Two. Gasping for air, I dropped my coffee cup on the wooden floor, murmuring, "Oh my God." My thoughts quickly leaped to the people I knew who worked on the 105th floor of Tower One. What was going through their heads? How would they safely escape the flames and smoke billowing from this horrible accident?

Meanwhile, Flight 93 had taken off from Newark Airport in New Jersey with thirty-three passengers, five crew members, and two pilots, scheduled to land about five hours later in San Francisco. Instead, four terrorists had hijacked that plane, planning to fly it directly into the Capitol Building in Washington, DC.

However, the actions of a few of the passengers and crew changed that plan, diverting Flight 93 to crash in a field just outside of Shanksville, Pennsylvania, less than twenty minutes from the terrorists' intended target. No one survived. A recording of what happened in the cockpit, combined with loved ones' accounts of phone conversations with the passengers, detailed the passengers' planned attack to take control back from the terrorists and prevent them from achieving their goal.[1]

As they prepared, Todd Beamer, one of the passengers, said a prayer and recited Psalm 39 while his wife listened via phone. They were ready.

"Let's roll," he said.

---

1 Michael Kaplan, "Let's Roll: The Heroic Final Moments of United Flight 93 on 9/11," The New York Post, September 11, 2020, accessed at https://nypost.com/2020/09/11/documentary-tells-new-details-of-9-11-flight-93-heroics/.

To this day, the words "let's roll" send chills up my spine. My mind occasionally wanders off to what it must have been like for the passengers on Flight 93. With this cry of retaliation, those brave passengers began the coup that prevented an incomprehensible amount of destruction and loss of lives.

What gave this group of passengers the courage to act? Had they learned something throughout their lives or experienced events that allowed them the tools needed to "roll"? Where did they draw this strength? Was this natural, or had they learned it? Do we all possess this ability?

I'd like to think that Split-Second Courage exists in each of us, but I imagine that the few passengers who led this charge had learned at least some of the skills to tap into their own when they needed it. While it may have only taken a moment for them to act, somehow, these passengers already knew how to unlock their highest potential. As you read on, I challenge you to push yourself to unlock your own Split-Second Courage.

Let's roll!

Introduction

"If you are going through hell, keep going."
—WINSTON CHURCHILL

It was 7:00 a.m.

The much-anticipated sunrise illuminated the mountain trail, dissolving all the shadowy threats that had lurked throughout the night. Twenty-five hours earlier, I had descended this steep mountainside cliff to embark on the journey of a lifetime. After enduring a grueling night of cold, pouring rain and mind-altering darkness, I still held tightly to an indefatigable spirit. I knew it was time to face my destiny. Mile ninety-nine consisted of a steep climb up a muddy, treacherous mountainside that seemed to touch the heavens. I was exhausted. I had nothing left in the tank, but I knew how to deal with that.

"Remember what you have been through, Christine," I repeated out loud. "Remember that this is all mental…this is all about mindset. You have survived much worse than this in your life.

This is just a little hill. One foot in front of the other."

Right. Left. Right. Left. Right…almost there.

Let. It. In.

Feel all the feels.

Embrace the pain.

Allow those dark thoughts of quitting, and begin to embrace weaknesses. Maybe you are not deserving.

Enter that "dark place" where you are never enough, and your insecurities are holding you back from achieving your dreams.

Take a good look around this terrible place. Now that you are there, take a deep breath. Go ahead.

Start counting backward from 10.

"10, 9, 8, 7, 6, 5, 4, 3, 2, 1..."

Right. Left. Right. Left. Right....

It only takes a split second to make a decision. But without courage, you won't make it—and without determination, you won't keep making it until you've achieved the goal.

Building both courage and determination can take a lifetime. It took me almost forty years to discover my true identity and understand my purpose in life. If not for the preceding events, I would have never learned the secrets that helped me grow my courage to act and attack my goals in life. I want to shortcut that process for you, so you don't have to wait that long.

Before continuing your journey to Split-Second Courage, you need to know a few essential things:

1. Split-Second Courage is something you can learn.
2. Everyone possesses the power to grow a more courageous mindset.

3. You deserve to live a meaningful life.
4. You deserve to be happy.

As you read on and reflect upon the powerful stories of everyday people's Split-Second Courage, think about how you can use these tools in your own life. Keep an open mind about this process and take tons of notes along the way. With practice and application, these tools will come in handy when you least expect them to. So go ahead; reach for the stars! Go live that fulfilling life that you have always dreamt of.

CHAPTER 1

'I Quit!'

"You have two choices in life. Do something or do nothing. Always choose something."
—WONDER WOMAN

WHEN I TURNED THIRTY-EIGHT, I QUIT.

I quit my safe, lucrative job; I quit superficial friendships; and I even quit my mother for a while until we could repair our relationship.

I also quit being angry all the time and taking it out on my family. I quit using alcohol to ease the pain of not allowing myself to forgive and move on. I quit hiding the fact that "being okay" was not okay, and I also quit "trying to fit in when I was born to stand out." (Thank you for that reminder, Dr. Seuss.)

An onlooker might have assumed I was experiencing what some refer to as an "early mid-life crisis." However, to me, this was the first time in my life that I felt truly alive. Although the sun was not shining more brightly, nor did I see any unicorns or rainbows, I did feel something that I had never felt before. For the first time, I allowed myself to let go, "feel all the feels," and accept what I could not control. I unapologetically spoke up for myself, celebrated my hardships as gifts, did what scared me, and embraced the fear. I finally realized how to draw courage from my past and unlock the door to the cell I had built around myself. Finally, after all those years, I emerged.

The source of all this happiness was not at all what you'd expect.

Quitting, Part 1

Many years prior, I sat, waiting. The crinkly, white parchment paper rustled as I nervously shifted my weight back and forth on the doctor's examining table. Time seemed to move backward as I tried to recall a few quick prayers from my Catholic upbringing before the stern knock at the door jolted me back to reality. As the silver doorknob slowly turned, I inhaled one last deep breath and adjusted my posture in anticipation for what was to come.

Taking a quick seat a few feet from my elevated table, the doctor began her litany: a long list of unidentifiable medical terminology, meaningless numbers, and various percentages, none of which meant anything to me. As she approached the final page of this seemingly endless document, she slowed her pace before reading the diagnosis: At the age of thirty-one, I had advanced rheumatoid arthritis.

RA is an aggressive autoimmune disease. My body was attacking itself, and nothing was off-limits. Visions of Grandma Jeanne, condemned to an oversized silver wheelchair for life, caused my breathing to hasten. She had received this same diagnosis more than fifty years ago. In my perception, it had been her death sentence. She had been unable to eat, clean herself, use the bathroom, get dressed, or even sit upright by herself.

As my mind roiled with these visions, my eyesight narrowed, and my hearing began to fade. I felt lightheaded and woozy.

Tears welled, streaming down my face like drops from a leaky faucet, and my nose started to run. Pins and needles formed at the tips of my fingers and toes as I unsuccessfully tried to take some deep breaths. The world seemed to be collapsing around me.

Doctor "So-and-So" (her name has blurred through the years) walked towards me with an unwelcome facial tissue.

"Why are you upset?" she asked. "It is just a positive diagnosis." She had the most uncomforting voice I have ever heard. Even my mother, known for her crass remarks, did not possess half the iciness this woman displayed. "Many people with your diagnosis can limit their activity and take medications to live many years functioning independently," she added, as if that should console me.

"Functioning independently?" I replied. "That is not my ultimate goal in life."

As Doctor Doom contributed to my heightened sense of despair, the tears of fright, of enormous loss, of my perceived death sentence flowed uncontrollably.

This moment would haunt me for the rest of my life.

During the dark months following my diagnosis, the ominous future of hardships I created in my mind pulled me deeper and deeper into a state of heightened anxiety, fear, and loss. I imagined a fate worse than death: a life of dependency, constant medications, doctor visits, compounding sicknesses, and eventually the slow and painful deterioration of my body. Just like that, my positive and hopeful outlook on life began to fade.

I drew inward; I stopped smiling; I cried often; and I began to lose faith.

"What on earth have I done to deserve this?" I thought. "Maybe if I were a better person, this wouldn't have happened."

That is when I decided I would rather die than live a life of captivity and become a physical, emotional, and financial burden to my husband, family, and friends.

I decided to quit.

It would be better than going on. I had already determined that.

This situation was not the only time in my life when I contemplated suicide. I knew the warning signs well, and this time wasn't much different.

While I put on a good show for those around me, I felt life was passing me by. It was as though I was watching television with the channel stuck on reruns of Dr. Phil, and I already knew the inevitable fate of the guests.

Day after day, I felt as though I was merely existing. I was going through the motions, waiting for my legs, arms, or lungs to suddenly start malfunctioning. Why wait for the pain? If all went as planned, my life insurance policy would kick in, allowing my husband and infant son the financial security to live happy lives. They could thrive, chase their dreams, and avoid the sacrifices of caring for an invalid.

Yes. It sounded better and better for everyone. The plans were in the works.

Quitting, Part 2

Shortly after I decided to "quit my life," I received a phone call that would yet again change the course of events.

It was 9:28 a.m. on a hot August morning. I was at the gym, about to begin my Sunday step aerobics sculpting class for a highly energetic group of women. As I adjusted the stereo, organized my choreography notes, and made last-minute adjustments to my headset, my phone lit up in my bag.

As usual, I ignored the phone and went into "upbeat instructor mode," making my routine pre-class safety announcements and offering motivational quotes. However, as I turned around and prepared to hit "play" on the stereo, I noticed my phone light up once again. Instinctively, I reached down to turn it off only to see that I had already missed two calls from my mother, who never called more than once.

Instead of turning it off, I hit "accept."

The news she gave me rocked my soul with that strange kind of out-of-body experience that comes with events like this. It transformed me into a bystander watching my very own horror movie.

My breathing became labored, my stomach somersaulted, and I became lightheaded and speechless. Time stopped.

My father had died.

A sickening feeling swept over me like an unforgiving tidal wave engulfing a small town.

My priorities immediately shifted.

Today, I would not be that energetic, inspirational fitness cheerleader to the room full of women. I would also not continue selfishly planning to end my own life. Instead, I would be thinking about those who were still alive. For them, I would transform myself. I would become a supportive daughter to my grieving mother, an empathetic listener to my two older sisters, and an example of strength for everyone who needed it. This priority trumped all others and marked the beginning of what I refer to as my "line in the sand."

Three days passed, after which four heartbroken women found themselves sitting uncomfortably in deep armchairs around an immense antique oak table at the funeral parlor. Living in different parts of the country and busy juggling careers and raising children, we rarely had moments such as these when we were all together in the same room. The air reeked of lilies, or what I like to refer to as "flowers of death," since they were a staple at every funeral I have attended.

Armed with a huge, ominous binder, an older man in a dark suit quietly entered the room and took a seat at the head of the long table. It was time to pick out my father's casket, a gut-wrenching experience that pains me to write. As I tried to function through this dreadful scene, my sisters became visibly upset, while Carol, my mother, remained stoic.

The funeral director asked what I assume to be the usual questions about caskets.

"What type and color of wood or metal do you prefer? What type of material and color scheme would you like on the inside? What is your budget?" he asked in a quiet, monotone voice.

The questions seemed endless. I could not help but think about how my dad had always joked that if anything happened to him, he'd want to be cremated and give his ashes to some seals and sea turtles. Let's just say that I kept that thought to myself since the air had grown uncomfortably thick with sadness and loss.

However, something happened then. I don't exactly know what came over me or what made me say it. I'd like to think that I channeled my dad's ability to lighten any mood with his slapstick and often inappropriate humor. He was known to crack jokes during grace, shoot you a funny face at church, laugh if you tripped, or even attack you with a fish-shaped oven mitt if you got close enough while he was cooking his famous crabs in the kitchen.

It just came out.

"Thank God I wore my Wonder Woman underwear today," I remarked. "Lord knows we could all use the strength of a superhero to get through this." While my sisters barely reacted to my attempt to provide some levity to this terrible situation, little did I know that my remark had unleashed the Kraken.

With Satan-like vengeance, my mother practically levitated from her chair and began the most vicious verbal attack I had ever experienced. In all fairness, I do not know if my grieving mother even remembers the powerfully hurtful, immensely degrading, and intentionally spiteful words that spewed from her mouth, but I will never forget them. They sparked something in me that had lain dormant until that moment.

What I have now come to understand as Split-Second Courage flowed through my veins like lava. My mind flashed back to many moments in quick succession—moments in which I had experienced cruelty yet had done nothing about it. That cold doctor's office where I sat weeping atop the examination table on that crinkly white paper. I remember wanting to lash out at that doctor for her lack of compassion and robotic and vapid bedside manner, but I did nothing.

Then my thoughts traveled to a different time—"that night." I was a young teenager. It was warm; it was extremely late at night; and I did not want to.

"No," I quietly repeated over and over. "Please, don't. No. No. That hurts. No. I don't...." became my chorus. I wanted to scream for help, stand up for myself, and fight back. I stood before my floor-length mirror on many occasions, for many, many years afterward, and cried.

But I did nothing.

My mind flashed to another scene—myself in my sixth-grade elementary school classroom. I was quietly sitting at my desk, completing my assignments as directed. Some students in the back of the room were throwing little pink erasers at me while speaking loudly enough for me to hear their derogatory slurs.

"Why is she so much bigger than the rest of us?" I heard. "She's my first pick to win the shot-put event at field day, but she would probably get disqualified because of the anabolic steroids she takes."

I remember trying desperately not to allow anyone in class see the tears that welled up in my eyes each day at their relentless, crushing teasing. I always wanted to stand up for myself. But instead, I took off my glasses with the big blue plastic frames and put them back on again, over and over, pretending to clean the lenses.

And I did nothing.

It suddenly occurred to me that in cases such as these throughout most of my life, I had always done nothing.

But that was about to end.

Fully awake with fire in my soul, I was back at that funeral home. In a split second, I woke up. I was ready to fight.

What followed was a scene somewhat resembling the one in *Superman II* where General Zod, Ursa, and Non were pummeling

Superman with deadly lasers in the Fortress of Solitude. Try as they might, the villains could not prevail against the superhero's strength and mental fortitude. On one knee, with one arm extended, Superman deflected the onslaught, eventually overcoming them by turning their weapons inward.

I withstood the slew of insults, just as Superman had. Sitting at that ominous table, I suddenly realized my courage was inside me all along. I just needed the right "cocktail" of experiences to bring it out. For me, this was quite the lightbulb moment. While for me, this moment happened unexpectedly, it doesn't have to. As you read on, you will learn how to bring about your own similar moments intentionally.

At that moment, I realized that I was my own version of Wonder Woman. I just had to find her, understand her, and believe in her.

Because the funny thing was, I really *was* wearing Wonder Woman underwear that day. One of my girlfriends had given them to me. After she spotted them at the store, she told me, "I had to buy these for you because a superhero must have matching panties."

This underwear represented my values, my ethics, and the "yes you can" mindset I embodied. They symbolized the friendships, laughs, support, and love that I shared among those in my life. They represented the willingness to #KFG, or "keep f'ing going," when life gets hard.

Like a superhero's unparalleled powers, my vision and hearing sharpened, my olfactory sense kicked into overdrive, and my mind cleared. I was no longer sitting in that suffocating funeral home feeling like I would never be "good enough." I was sitting there shopping for my father's dreadful coffin with my eyes wide open.

For the first time in my life, I understood what Dr. Seuss wrote about when he said,

"Why fit in when you were born to stand out?"

What happened next might have appeared rather anticlimactic to an onlooker.

No shouting matches occurred; no one flipped the tables in fury; I didn't storm out of the room and slam the door. In fact, you would have had to listen hard to hear the simple "No," that escaped my lips as my eyes squinted, finally seeing past all of the walls I had built around myself for so many years. My mind racing, I tried to hold back newly forming tears. These were no longer just the tears of sadness for the passing of my father. Instead, they marked a different kind of mourning—and more importantly, a new dawn. What happened was mostly internal, and it was a decision.

For most people, underwear choice may not lead to life-altering experiences, but that day, it made a world of difference. After that day, I began to wear those Wonder Woman underwear mentally every day, even if I wasn't wearing them physically. I was finally ready to start unapologetically revealing my true identity to the world.

That day I proudly quit "doing nothing" and became the inner superhero I had always wished I was.

I would no longer miss opportunities due to self-doubt, insecurity, or fear. I would no longer allow myself to carry around the guilt and shame of past events that were not my fault. I would no longer worry about what or who I could not control, but instead, I would stand up and face all that I had once feared. It was time to speak up, rise up, and boldly run towards the life I deserved.

After that day, I made one decision after another from this new self-awareness. And like a slow avalanche gaining speed, each courageous decision made the next one even more effortless. Relentless and determined, I watched my old life begin to fall away and become a blur of dust in the distance.

Quitting, Part 3

Shortly after the sudden passing of my father, a cute couple in their early thirties named Chuck and Mindy began attending my weekly fitness classes at a local facility.

Each week, they came in together, took class side-by-side, and worked hard. However, one October day, they failed to show up for their scheduled morning class. Though missing a session was out of the ordinary for them, I wasn't concerned. They both worked in medicine, were on active duty in the military, and parented a four-year-old, and I assumed one of these elements had taken precedence over the class that week.

Shortly after, I received the message that the couple would need to freeze their memberships due to a family emergency. Although I didn't have a relationship with them outside of the training environment, my practice was to check in on my clients to make sure they were okay and let them know we missed them. However, before I even had the chance to call, my manager told me that Chuck had suddenly passed away.

Five days later, I walked into Chuck's wake and found a seat among a sea of police officers, men in military uniforms, and more than a hundred other friends and family of the couple. I inhaled deeply. The pungent smell of lilies immediately conjured forty years' worth of mental still-frames of coffins, grief, tears, and saying goodbye to grandparents, parents, aunts and uncles, friends, and former students through my life.

However, this situation was different. Surveying the room, I saw not the expected grief and tears but instead the faces of confused, angry, hurt, and even vengeful people.

I looked up at the giant television screen repeating a beautiful montage of images: Chuck, smiling with his wife and daughter at Disney World, Chuck happily pushing a stroller, and many other scenes in which he is living a joyful, fulfilling life. I even did a double-take as a picture of Mindy, Chuck, and myself flashed across the screen, displaying a trifecta of smiles suggesting a bright future of positivity and health.

Finally, I spotted Mindy. She wore a beautiful, simple black dress. Our eyes met. I approached her and gave my usual "funeral offering," which consisted of a hug and the assurance that I was sending tons of positive energy and love to her and her family.

"What are you doing here?" she said, her eyes wide in surprise.

"What do you mean?" I replied flippantly, trying to lighten the mood. "I wouldn't miss this for the world! I love wakes. I actually wake-hop on Wednesdays. It's my thing." I figured she needed a little levity in this dark moment.

Then my tone became more serious. "In my world, when you know someone who is going through some 'stuff,' you show up," I explained.

That's how I see it. It may sound a bit dark and twisty, but I am a "funeral person." If a friend or co-worker experiences a loss, I always show up to the wake or funeral. It matters! I will never forget those friends who spent hours driving to New York to console me with hugs and sympathetic tears after my father's passing.

I will also never forget those who I thought would be there for me and never showed.

Less than two weeks later, a newly widowed Dr. Mindy returned to her weekly workout session. It was now her turn to "show up." Later that day, she came to see me and told me a story that would remain with me for the rest of my life.

The happy, successful, caring, and healthy man—the father, husband, friend, and hard worker Chuck had displayed to the world—was not as he seemed.

In disbelief, I tried to hold back tears as Dr. Mindy, unusually calm and matter-of-fact, described the gruesome details of Chuck's suicide. While she and their four-year-old daughter were away for the night, Chuck chose to end his life in their family's home with an unforgiving bullet to the head. Secretly suffering from deep-seated post-traumatic stress disorder (PTSD) and the unrelenting side effects of depression (possibly from his military service), Chuck successfully implemented and executed his plan. Mindy found him after and had to shield their daughter from the brunt of the situation. Their daughter still cries out for her father, still wants to know why he left them, and will forever be left with the question, "Why?"

That afternoon, I got into my car and cried. I cried for the loss of a life and the loss of a father, a husband, and a friend. I cried because I understood what he must have been going through. I cried at the thought of how much pain he must have been in to believe that he was not worthy enough to live. I cried because I, too, understood some of the emotions he must have been feeling, which enabled him to create and execute his plan.

When I got home that night, I sat before the TV, neither seeing nor hearing the broadcast. I sipped my usual glass of Pinot Noir but tasted nothing, my mind elsewhere. I could not stop thinking about the suicide—the lifelong grief and heartache Chuck had left for his wife and daughter.

The questions remained. What type of Split-Second Courage was missing from Chuck's life that could have helped him put the gun down? And what other kind of Split-Second Courage did he possess that made him pull the trigger?

I couldn't quit thinking, but I did quit one thing altogether that night—I never again thought about taking my own life.

Reflection: Do You Need Split-Second Courage?

1. Why did you choose to read *Split-Second Courage*? What do you expect to gain from it?
2. How often in life have you been faced with a decision to "do something, or do nothing?"
3. Are you armed with the tools needed to act on your decision?
4. What have you "quit" in your life? Was it worth it?
5. What are you willing to "quit"? What do you think it might bring you?
6. What prevents you from quitting the "thing" that is holding you back from achieving your dreams?

CHAPTER 2

What is 'Split-Second Courage'?

WE HAVE ALL BEEN THERE.

You want to speak up for yourself or against someone or something that you disagree with, but you don't. How many times have you seen a parent mistreat their child in public? How many fights have you witnessed? How many times have you stood on the sidelines in your own life rather than stepping up? Why didn't you take that trip you always wanted to go on? Why didn't you ask that person out? Why didn't you ask for that promotion? What were you afraid of? Why didn't you "be the change"?

Why didn't you *act*?

What if I ...
I wish I would have ...
Imagine if I ...
I wonder what my life would be like if I ...

If you opened this book, you are somehow intrigued by the phrase "Split-Second Courage." You may be asking yourself whether you have this capability, and if so, whether/how you have displayed it in your life. You may even be trying to create your own definition of Split-Second Courage as it relates to your personal relationship with courage. In actuality, Split-Second Courage is a type of knee-jerk reaction based on a complicated juxtaposition of events, experiences, and emotions. All of these come together and lead you to create a line in the sand—in other words, you quit.

What your "line in the sand" ends up looking like depends on your own decision. It can be a positive decision that empowers you to overcome a challenge and do something extraordinary. Or it can be a negating decision to opt out of life entirely, as Chuck did.

In either case, you quit making excuses, listening to your fears, or letting the bully take advantage of you. Yet...which one brings about something better for you and the others around you? Which one shows you more "yes you can" in the long run?

It takes more courage to quit your fear than it does to let your fear quit you.

By nurturing your empowering Split-Second Courage, you grant yourself the ability to step outside your comfort zone and take more calculated risks. Trying more things and acting on opportunities more often can enable you to live a truly fulfilling and successful life. Think about it this way: professional athletes continually practice their sport. Medical professionals spend years in school, and artists devote their lives to perfecting their work. In the same way, honing Split-Second Courage takes days, months, years, decades, and even a lifetime. The most important thing to realize is that you have had this capability inside you all along. In that knowledge, you will, at last, be able to set both it—and yourself—free.

One of my good friends, Joel Matalon, refers to Split-Second Courage as the ability to recognize "skydiving moments" in life. When you jump out of the plane, you do so with the tools necessary to react and cope with the decision—that is, if you free yourself from what is holding you back from jumping in the first place.

Fear, self-doubt, and self-deprecating or closed mindsets are everyday human experiences, and they can hold you back. However, when you use the proper "Split-Second Courage (SSC) Tools," you can harness doubts and overcome fear. As your courage grows, your "SSC Meter" will also level up. As you grow accustomed to making bold decisions, you will take on even more daunting situations and live a more fulfilling life. (You will learn more about the SSC Meter in chapter 7.)

It all starts with your reason for deciding in the first place.

The 'Why' Factor

Nothing riles me up more than a show called *What Would You Do?*

This hybrid reality television show has been around for decades. Using hidden cameras, it establishes everyday scenarios to capture people's reactions and reveal whether they choose to respond or mind their own business when they experience a wrongful act. This show really depicts a person's SSC Meter—how much will they take before acting?

Having Split-Second Courage isn't as simple as it may seem. It requires you to analyze a situation, decide the appropriate action, know whether you can handle the consequences, and then act—all in a single moment. The show depicts people doing these things.

For me, watching it is pure torture.

I am sure I am not the only one who talks to the television for whatever reason. I voice the occasional expletive when I disagree with the meteorologist's weekend forecast. I may shout a few choice words when my alma mater, the University of Maryland, is losing a basketball game (Go Terps!). However, *What Would You Do?* wins for the number of objections I'm known to hurl at the screen during any given episode.

How and why would anyone choose *not* to help an old lady pick up the groceries strewn around on the street after her grocery bag ripped? Why wouldn't someone speak up when they see someone physically or emotionally abusing a young child? Why wouldn't a person do something if they noticed someone shoplifting? These are just a few examples of the countless scenarios this show has paraded before me each week—situations that rattle my brain forever after.

Why *wouldn't* you speak up for yourself in any wrongful situation? *What is it* that pulls some to act almost on instinct while others passively sit back and watch? Why do some people have more Split-Second Courage than others? Does it have to do with their past experiences and resiliency? Is it something more?

I already knew the answer, but I just hadn't realized it yet.

The Real Story of Peter Pan

It was the first day of fifth grade. Jenny's platinum-blond Peter Pan haircut made her appear almost angelic—that is, however, until she opened her mouth. She was outspoken, funny, crass, energetic, and quite the rabble-rouser. The saying that opposites attract is true, and we instantaneously became the best of friends. She was the peanut butter to my jelly.

Jenny consistently got into trouble for speaking her mind, not completing her work, or cracking inappropriate jokes in class. I, on the other hand, played the role of the good girl. I always followed the rules, always had my work done, and always got the "lucky" desk position next to the "bad kid" because I was "mature enough" to handle it. Or so I was told.

We remained friends over the ensuing years, during which I continued to be the "good girl," and Jenny continued being her unpredictable, unapologetic self. I thought I was happy with the role I had chosen, but inside, I was so jealous of Jenny's fearlessness and her refusal to take anyone's shit!

Was she just born that way? Maybe in part, but that wasn't the whole explanation. I always knew there was a certain mystique about Jenny, but it wasn't until many years later that I understood why she could harness Split-Second Courage at such a young age.

Unfortunately, I had to experience something horrific to find out.

Flash forward to ninth grade, a night four years after Jenny came into my life. It must have been about 2:00 a.m. The house was quiet. Aside from the low hum from the window air conditioning units nearby, I could almost make out the lapping of the water against the bulkhead in the backyard. It was a warm July night, but the cool breeze that flowed through the small bathroom window brought a faint reminder of the impending fall season. It signaled the end of yet another summer, which would bring me one year closer to adult independence.

As I stood there in an oversized T-shirt and Gap boxer shorts—the fashion of the times—my reflection in the mirror did not appear any different from the previous hour. No new bruises or scratches marred my skin. I showed no signs of struggle. Aside from the slow raindrops of blood that intermittently fell to the tile floor, I was fine.

Those "fine" eyes, however, true windows to the soul, told a vastly different story—one that would forever haunt every fiber of my being. This night would not be the last one in which those "fine" eyes would stare into that mirror and wonder: "Why?"

Why did I not have the courage to say something?
What am I afraid of?
Why was I not more assertive? Why did my "no's" go unheard?
This is all my fault.

The man had come through my window. Unprepared, I did not know what to do. He had taken me by surprise.

Throughout the following weeks, I endured extreme bouts of shame, depression, worthlessness, and disgust about what I had let happen. However, I also came to learn something that surprised me.

That same unwelcome man had stealthily slipped through Jenny's second-story window and into her bed, too. However, Jenny's story turned out quite differently from mine.

She told me everything. Suave and intimidating, the man coveted the same irreplaceable thing he had stolen from me.

But to his surprise, he was no match for her.

She was not afraid to tell him no. She was not afraid to call for help or to fight back. She didn't care whether he thought she was a "good girl" and obedient and apologetic.

And now, as Jenny revealed the stories of her childhood experiences, I learned the reasons she had this arsenal of weapons with which to fight him. She had already endured things that rivaled anything he could have done to her.

The year before Jenny had come into my life, she and her younger sister had been captives in a small closet in a dirty apartment for more than a week. During that time, their only nourishment consisted of some fruit cups their drug-addicted mother and her disgusting human being of a boyfriend occasionally threw into the closet.

These two sisters knew only abuse, neglect, suffering, and pain. That closet was their bedroom, their bathroom, their only reality.

Then Aunt Jill stepped in.

In her early twenties and newly married, Aunt Jill was a whirlwind. She swept into that foul-smelling apartment and ripped Jenny and her sister out of captivity with a vengeance. She didn't think; she acted—one of the most moving displays of Split-Second Courage I have ever come across to this day.

She took those girls into her home, showed them what it was like to be loved, and began to raise them as her own. This new family then moved to my small town on the south shore of Long Island a few weeks before the start of the school year. That was when Peter Pan came into my life and showed me what it would be like to be the person I wished I could be. She had only found that person in herself after going through sheer hell, and she was not about to lose what she had gained from that experience—her own Split-Second Courage.

When the man tried to take advantage of her as he had me, Jenny already possessed the tools that freed her from his expectations. She was not afraid to speak, she didn't fear what others would think, and she would never again let anyone "lock her in a closet." Her voice was loud and powerful, and she defended herself relentlessly. You see, Jenny wasn't afraid of getting in trouble, tarnishing her reputation, or bringing shame to her family. She was a survivor and a fighter, and her painful past was her tool to find Split-Second Courage in any situation.

The 'Permission' Conundrum

Like Jenny, many of us have been through painful situations that have taught us tons of valuable life lessons. However, many people will experience obstacles and endure hardships but will still not permit themselves to act. Why is this? Why do some people grant themselves permission to "just do it," while others shy away from any uncomfortable situations?

I imagine the answers go back to the "line in the sand," the boundary between the two types of permission. Either we permit others to continue doing what they're doing unchallenged, or we authorize ourselves to act to prevent those actions.

This process happens differently in each person. We all have different "lines," based on the kind of situations we're in and the permissions we've given ourselves to act within them. For instance, by the time I reached the last few months of my teaching career, I had come a long way from being the young, unprepared, unassertive girl on that long-ago summer night. Yet, I didn't realize quite how much I'd changed until I encountered a different kind of horrifying situation.

I had twenty minutes to grab lunch. Surely, I could gas up my car, make it through the Dunkin' Donuts drive-through for my daily butter pecan iced coffee and chocolate chip muffin (try not to judge my nutritious lunch choice until you teach a hundred teenagers English each day) and get back in time for my curtain call.

It seemed like one of those days where everything was running like a well-oiled machine. The sun was shining, and the birds may have even been chirping. The drive-through experience was flawless, and the gas station attendant came right over as I pulled in. I would have plenty of time.

As I sat in my driver's seat waiting for my tank to fill, a sound slashed through the perfect summer's day, making my heart race. No more than twenty-five feet away, just past some low hedges, two vehicles had smashed together in a head-on collision in the center of the main intersection.

Glass, oil, gas, smoke, and plastic particles spilled out onto the concrete around the scene. One light-blue caravan lay teetering on its side with its horn blaring uncontrollably. A dust cloud emerged from its deployed airbags, and lifeless passengers were dangling from their seatbelts, looking eerily like crash-test dummies. In the adjacent car, a blood-covered gentleman with short silver hair fumbled with his door handles, trying to break free from the mangled metal that had been an attractive sedan.

It all happened so fast. I don't even remember running from my car while it was gassing up. I left the driver's side door wide open, my pocketbook on the front seat, and the keys in the ignition. I recall hobbling across the street in my "teacher clothes"—brown wedge sandals and one of my favorite long skirts that constricted my ability to move quickly. It could not have taken more than thirty seconds to reach the blood-covered man limping out of his sedan.

Others suddenly appeared to help break the windows to extract the lifeless passengers in the toppled caravan. I was the first to reach the older man, who was clearly in shock and unsure what happened or how badly he was injured. I was the only one attending to him. Blood ran out from a gash across his forehead like a slow waterfall. One of his shoulders seemed dislocated, and all his knucklebones in both hands were exposed.

I carefully maneuvered him to the side of the road and sat him down beside a large wooden telephone pole before running back to my car. Returning quickly with rags, disinfecting wipes, tissues, and a water bottle, I knelt on the uneven gravel. I reached down for his wrist to check his heart rate and covered the exposed bones in his hands protruding through the skin. His heart raced as he sat there and shook from the shock of what had just happened.

"What is your name? How old are you? Where are you experiencing pain?" I asked.

His trembling body emitted a quiet, "Daniel," and then came the unforgettable monotonous moaning. "Oh my God, please tell me those people will be okay," he cried. Apparently, he had caused the wreck by running a red light.

As I knelt by Daniel's side, trying to distract him from the gruesome wreck, I witnessed an incredible example of Split-Second Courage. At least twelve men of all ages, dressed in everything from business suites to maintenance uniforms, had gathered in the intersection. They were shattering the windows and extricating people from that side-lying caravan, which had now begun to gush gasoline. The men dragged each of the four passengers one by one from the wreckage and lined them up on the side of the road a safe distance from the scene. Finally, sirens blared, announcing the arrival of ambulances and police.

The medics approached.

"Daniel, I know you are in good hands, and you are going to be okay," I assured him.

As they catered to Daniel's open wounds, I couldn't help but take a deep breath and take in what had just happened. In those last twenty minutes, superheroes emerged from what seemed like thin air, equipped with an arsenal of tools to act immediately without thinking or worrying. None of those heroes seemed to display any doubt or fear as they worked together to rescue those trapped passengers. While I will never know the identity of those heroes, I do know that each of those men shared a deep understanding of how to implement Split-Second Courage in their lives.

Yet all of that begs the question. It's true that we all have the potential to execute SSC decisions. Yet, we also each have selective "permissions" that, for whatever reason, we elect to give ourselves in some cases while not in others. So, the question is, what's behind these internal permissions? Is our objection to taking authority really as important as we believe it is? How is it holding us back from things that we need or want to do, and why?

In this situation, all of us had unchallenged permission to act. I had launched into motion the moment I saw that someone needed help. I didn't have to think about it. I didn't wait for the authorities to come and take care of everything. In this case, I decided to be an "authority." So did those men. Yet, someone else might not have done so in the same situation.

And do all those men, who were superheroes during the accident, have that kind of Split-Second Courage in every situation? Knowing that they are human, too, I would suspect not. I'm sure they struggle with internal obstacles in other instances where they aren't sure whether they should act. Some actions are natural, while others aren't. These differ from one person to another.

And I wonder: As unsure and afraid to act in certain situations as my younger self was, would she have hesitated to leap out of her car and help the man?

It was a totally different kind of situation, and I might have had other "permissions" for it. When people's lives were in danger, or they were hurt and needed care, I may have been "authorized" to act, even back then.

It takes self-reflection to understand why certain things are unquestionably "okay" to do in your internal makeup while others are not. But once you start discovering your own answers, you can reconnect your internal wiring to take a different path—with new permissions. Doing that is a key step toward achieving SSC within all the areas in your life where it can benefit you.

And this is an ongoing process. It may only take a split second to make a decision, but retraining yourself to make courageous decisions in different situations takes constant practice throughout your life. As you learn more about Split-Second Courage through the stories you read in this book, remember that attaining this type of courage involves reflecting on personal experiences.

These experiences provide lessons that help us not only find our inner strength, but also identify and eliminate the obstacles to our "permission." Only then can we implement and execute Split-Second Courage throughout all aspects of our lives.

Reflection: What Is Split-Second Courage?

1. Have you experienced a "locked in the closet" event in your life? If so, how did you get out of it?
2. How did this event change your view on life? How did it affect your decision-making?
3. Can you remember how you felt before, during, and after this experience? Compare those feelings. Did you change in any way? How?
4. Have you ever witnessed an accident or event where you immediately volunteered your assistance? If so, why did you feel you needed to act? If not, why did you elect not to act?
5. Name three experiences that have taught you something about what you would or would not do in an emergency (i.e., stay calm, cry, panic, help, run, etc.).
6. What did your reaction teach you or tell you about yourself?

CHAPTER 3

What is Holding You Back?

Did you ever stop and wonder why you didn't say "yes"?

"...BUT WHAT ABOUT YOUR PENSION?" my mother condescendingly, yet lovingly, questioned in her heavy Long Island accent.

Carol was worried because, at the age of thirty-eight, I had decided to take a sabbatical from my full-time job as a high school English teacher and varsity volleyball coach.

She herself had been a kindergarten teacher for thirty-nine years while simultaneously raising three girls, taking care of the house, making sure the bills were paid, getting dinner on the table each night, and ensuring we had a solid education. She was born in 1941 to first-generation immigrant children who had survived two world wars and experienced the hardships that accompanied the Great Depression. They had taught her to value their own parents' courage and sacrifices in leaving their poverty-stricken homes in Poland and Ireland to seek the American dream.

Due to her upbringing, Carol made sure to instill in my sisters and me the need to secure a career that provided financial independence, which was vital for living "the good life." However, it wasn't until my late thirties that I truly understood that living "the good life" might not mean what I was programmed to believe.

This teaching/coaching position was my second "I made it" career, and from an outsider's perspective, I probably looked like I had a fantastic life. I made great money, my hours were consistent, the benefits were phenomenal, and I had the flexibility to work full-time in the fitness industry every summer. We had a big house with a pool; we could pay the bills; and we could even afford family vacations and date nights here and there.

However, it wasn't *my* life.

From the inside, it looked completely different—and not so wonderful.

It was 6:30 a.m. Once again, I found myself sitting in my idling car in spot #31. The sun was not yet breaking the horizon, and my coffee was just not doing the trick. I was still half asleep.

It was going to be yet another day filled with lies.

I was a hypocrite. Each morning, after a self-coaching session that eventually led me to get out of the car and head into the school, I faced a day in which I would then have to pontificate to my students about the importance of following their dreams and passions.

"Only when you choose to follow your heart and surround yourself with those who lift you up and support you will you experience happiness and success," I preached.

For almost sixteen years, I taught thousands of young adults to steer clear of toxic environments, avoid chasing other people's dreams, and turn their obstacles into their greatest gifts. So just imagine the shock on their faces on their last day of class when I told them that it took me my whole life to take my own advice, and I would not be coming back.

A life inside four walls meant success for many, like my mother, but it was not my dream. To me, those walls were suffocating. Each morning as I closed the door to room 411, I knew something was missing. I knew I had a greater calling—and following that calling required Split-Second Courage.

I saw the line in the sand. I didn't think before walking down to the principal's office and resigning from my position. I just acted.

Routines Kill

How often has someone asked you how you were doing, and you responded by saying, "I'm fine"?

According to extraordinarily successful award-winning author and inspirational speaker Mel Robbins, this nasty little four-letter word is an obstacle. It holds you back from moving out of your comfort zone and feeding your soul. Lying to yourself and others about how you truly feel about your life, job, relationships, and happiness is a recipe for disaster, or at least a lifetime of complacency, unfulfillment, and boredom. False satisfaction directly opposes Split-Second Courage.

By nature, human beings crave feelings of comfort, safety, and belonging. When people face uncomfortable decisions or situations, they often respond like frightened turtles, retracting into their safe, protective inner shells. Rather than deciding to feed the soul and embrace "all the feels," they resign themselves to living lives where they are "fine."

But this is the equivalent of accepting mediocrity. What is the cost of that?

Suppose you are a carpenter, building a piece of furniture. You put every ounce of yourself into designing the piece, measuring the materials, carefully cutting and shaping each part, piecing it all together, sanding, staining, and polishing the surfaces. At the end, you proudly stand back and survey your work. You might not have done everything perfectly at first, but you learned things while doing the work that will help you perfect it next time. You know you put your whole self into it.

Now suppose you're another carpenter building a different piece of furniture. You don't want to take the time to measure, so you don't get the correct measurements. The parts don't fit together quite right, which makes you angry. Now it's going to take even more time! But you don't have time to rework them, and it doesn't matter anyway. The piece will still do its job even if it's not perfect. Besides, you don't really like building furniture anyway. You slap the project together, just wanting to get it done. Are you proud of the piece of furniture you've created?

When someone asks how the first carpenter's work is going, their answer would probably be full of enthusiasm—something like, "Oh, I'm building the most awesome table! The wood is just spectacular; it took hours to select just the right grain. The legs came out perfectly, and I got to use this new piece of equipment I just bought..."

But how would the second carpenter respond to the same question? If the response is not an expletive, it would probably be, "Fine." That's to spare you from the swearing.

I'm not even talking about whether someone else would buy the piece or how it would function for its purpose. How does the whole process make you feel when you're "not really into" it? And why settle for that feeling?

Not accepting being "okay" and not wanting to be just "fine" is necessary! On my classroom wall, I used to have a big gravestone that read, "RIP. We shall not use these limiting or vague words to describe our life or experiences." The words "stuff," "fine," and "hope" were my top three for decades. Be bold! Be specific!

The only way to do that is to know exactly who you are and what you want. Don't let others define these things for you or tell you when you should be "fine." Authorize yourself to make those decisions.

The Fear of '-Ing'

"Hey, Mom. Have you ever heard of The Fear of '-Ing'?" my seven-year-old daughter Lauren asked from the backseat of my Jeep on the way to her swim practice.

"The Fear of '-Ing'?" I replied, intrigued. "No. I have never heard of it. What is it?"

"So, we played this game in school today where we have to go around in a circle and come up with all the scary words that end in '-ing.' Do you want to play? I'll start: 'frightening,' 'screaming,' 'drowning,'" she proudly announced.

"Okay, how about, 'depressing,'" I replied.

"Great, Mom," she told me and then went on. "'Crying,' 'hurting,' 'killing'..."

"Wow," I said, "this game is really dark. Can we change the directions a bit? How about we name positive words that end in '-ing'? How about 'loving,' 'caring,' 'laughing,' and 'smiling'?"

"'Swimming,' 'splashing,' 'singing,'" Lauren contributed.

And just like that, the tone of the conversation changed. It was so simple. Flipping the negative "-ings" to positive "-ings" completely changed the mood and energy in that car. Until we arrived at swim practice, we continued to surround ourselves with uplifting, motivating, empowering, and affirming words.

The power of positive words and affirmations matters. Period. Take a moment and think about how often you play "The Fear of '-ing'" without even knowing it. Do you have a phone? If so, I guarantee you may be a master at this game.

Picture this: You are at your desk engulfed in that big project when your phone rings. Your blood pressure rises due to the unwanted interruption. Annoyed, your mind starts to theorize what kind of stressful phone conversation it will be. You just know it is someone with a trivial question or yet another unreasonable request. As you unwillingly answer, your disgruntled tone conveys negative energy to the caller even before you know who they are.

Does this ring a bell? How many times have you played this game? You have unconsciously collected all the negative "-ings." You were "judging, projecting, and concluding" that this experience was going to be "annoying, interrupting, bothering, and unfulfilling" even before knowing and engaging in the actual call. In fact, how many other situations have you been in where you prematurely projected all the negative "-ings"?

What impulsive "-ings" spring to mind when you encounter the following?

- A knock at the door?
- A request to meet with your boss?

- The arrival of your blind date?
- A long line at the drive-through?
- An unexpected flight delay?
- That Christmas present from Aunt Edna that is meowing?

The 'THINK'

I am not here to teach you what to think,
I am here to teach you how to think.
—MRS. CONTI, THE ENGLISH TEACHER

If you are reading this book, you likely suffer from something I call "The Think." When improperly diagnosed, this sneaky little ailment can pack a powerful punch to your Split-Second Courage.

The ability to think for yourself, analyze facts and data, and make educated choices can seem like a powerful tool. However, like any tool, when used in the wrong manner, it can cripple you. The Think will cause you to fixate not only on all the possible positive outcomes of your decision but also on all the possible negative outcomes as well. Decision-making becomes impossible.

Things such as changing careers or filing for divorce definitely require a lot of thought, but when The Think intrudes, the mental burden becomes unsurpassable. Even choosing whether you want lemon in your iced water becomes a stressful, mind-numbing process. You lay out spreadsheets in your head that contain detailed analyses and breakdowns of risk versus reward, return on investment, and even caloric intake versus expenditure. Your mind runs through this data repeatedly as if you didn't know that repeating the same thing over and over is the definition of insanity. You are neither moving forward nor regressing in your personal or professional life because when you come down with The Think, you aren't moving at all.

When clients ask me if I think they are ready to finally chase down their dreams, switch jobs, go on that vacation, or relocate, my answer always remains the same. STOP THINKING ABOUT IT! Less thinking, more doing.

Wonder Woman reminds us to "always choose something." That "something" leads to perpetual forward motion. No matter what, this will lead to significant growth. If you make a mistake—so what? You will make mistakes. It's part of developing more life experience to grow your Split-Second Courage for the future.

Are you someone who constantly doubts your decision-making skills? Do you find it hard to overcome The Think? If this describes you, it's okay! While changing your entire decision process will not happen overnight, you can start by voicing small instinctual decisions. For example, if someone asks, "How is your day?": instead of the generic answer of, "It's good," don't think about it and say the first thing that comes to mind.

"I'm really stressed out today. How are you?"

Or, "I am seriously having the best day ever. Someone paid for my coffee at Dunkin', and I just nailed my presentation. And you?"

Or, "My day quickly went to hell in a handbasket. I got rear-ended on the way to the office. Is your day any better?"

Not only are these responses authentic, but they also don't require any extra thinking *because they are true*. They aren't a PR statement made to keep your perfect image intact. They aren't a way to spare others from your actual being. Answers like these are low-risk ways to use Split-Second Courage to be true to yourself.

Not Thinking Saves Lives

It was a cold autumn night in upstate New York. I was a sophomore in college. After a night of party hopping and dancing until my feet were screaming, a group of us returned to campus just in time to order the most delectable, greasy, cheesy pizza in all of Binghamton. At 1:00 a.m., post pizza-annihilation, my pillow was calling my name. So, as usual, I trekked the two-hundred-foot walk up the long, wide cement stairs that joined the two immense brick dormitory buildings.

However, on this night, as I climbed the dark stairs to the landing where my dorm entrance was, I sensed that something was wrong. I heard yells, screams, cursing, racial slurs, and the sound of blunt force punches and swift kicks. I swiftly climbed the stairs while my stomach climbed into my throat.

Before me was a gruesome scene. Five shadowy images huddled tightly around one fallen, unresponsive Asian young man. The terrible group resembled wild animals. The punching, kicking, and spitting was something out of a wild, terrible nightmare that wouldn't stop, and no one else was in sight.

There I was, a young woman with no weapons and no time to think.

I ran without hesitation towards the fallen boy as his assailants landed a few last kicks to his head. I will never forget those eyes. They were stone cold, lifeless, bleeding, and unresponsive. I screamed. I don't remember what I was saying, but I knew I needed to draw attention to the terrible scene. My eyes remained vigilant, taking mental notes of the group of five men as they dispersed in different directions. I stayed on the ground, checking vitals until the medics arrived to take over.

Over twenty years have passed since that night, but I will never forget the rush that came over me when I abandoned The Think and acted upon instinct. Did I put myself into unnecessary danger? Did I have any business getting involved? Did I know that if I hadn't stepped in when I did, that boy on the ground would have died?

I don't care. I didn't take the time to worry about those things. The young man on the ground didn't have the time to award me that luxury. So instead, I chose to act.

"We think too much and feel too little."
—CHARLIE CHAPLIN

If you're feeling a little overwhelmed from reading about all the things that have been holding you back, don't worry. Through the next chapters, we'll explore science-based solutions that will get you back on track to achieve your goals. By implementing these SSC Tools and getting plenty of daily practice, you can overcome your inner obstacles and start moving toward a more fulfilling life.

Reflection: What Is Holding You Back?

1. Are people in your life holding you back? Who? Why?
2. If you had no concerns about money, how would your daily life be different?
3. Name your top three negative "-ings" and describe how they have held you back.
4. Name your top three positive "-ings" and how they improve the quality of your life.
5. How many times each day/week/month do you think you project a negative outcome before you even encounter the full situation? Try keeping track by carrying a notepad or recording them in your smartphone notes app.
6. What decisions have caused you to suffer most from The Think? Why?
7. What knee-jerk decisions have you made in life that required zero thinking? Why were they different? Did you regret any ramifications? If so, how might fear of making the same mistakes be holding you back in other situations?

CHAPTER 4

Split-Second Science

"I realize nobody's coming to save me. I must save myself.
I must be my own superhero.
Although I am open to a sidekick."
—KAREN SALMANSOHN

Hire the Right 'Assistant'

THE MOST SUCCESSFUL AND POWERFUL PEOPLE in the world have assistants. Presidents have vice presidents, managers have assistant managers, head coaches have assistant coaches, and even superheroes have sidekicks. Assistants are sometimes just as important, if not more so at times, in ensuring the mighty leader's success as they embark on any enterprise.

Assistants should be diligent, driven, and positive. Terrible assistants should be fired and immediately replaced, so they don't negatively affect the goals of the person in charge.

In short, your assistant is vital to your success.

"But Christine," you say, "I don't have an assistant. And I can't afford one."

But you do have one! And you've had one all along.

It's just that he/she is inside your head.

No, I'm not crazy, nor do I think you are. International No. 1 Bestselling author Nathalie Plamondon-Thomas was the first to speak about the analogy that everyone has an inner "Personal Assistant."[2] This inner assistant, whom some refer to as the unconscious mind or "that voice in your head," feeds us almost eighty-thousand thoughts per day.

The power of your inner assistant becomes relevant when you understand another shocking truth: Around 70 percent of our thoughts each minute are negative. Yes. Negative. We trash talk ourselves all day long. Seriously, it's no wonder we don't stand up to people like that jerk at the office who keeps asking us to cover for him while he ducks out early. Or that we don't say "yes" to that girls' or boys' weekend in Vegas because we worry about leaving Fluffy home alone.

Firing the inner assistant is not an option. It's not possible to get rid of that voice entirely. So, what do we do?

Will you accept a life of self-deprecation, self-doubt, and regret? Or will you learn to reprogram that inner assistant and grow Split-Second Courage?

In addition to her previously mentioned credentials, Nathalie Plamondon-Thomas is an international speaker and the founder and CEO of Think Yourself® Academy, though she is better known

2 "Think Yourself Academy." Nathalie Plamondon-Thomas, 2021, http://thinkyourselfacademy.com/.

as "the confidence expert." If you have yet to Google this powerful blond bombshell, time is wasting! Nathalie's fascination with neuroscience led her to discover groundbreaking techniques that could change negative self-talk and reprogram the inner Personal Assistant to be positive and supportive.

Conventional positive-thinking methods don't work because they aren't realistic. When you try to go directly from "I'm so stressed out" to "I am super calm," you create an affirmation that is suddenly overly positive. It describes the total opposite of what you are feeling, and unfortunately, your mind just doesn't buy it. It sounds like fiction, and your mind treats it as such.

Instead, Nathalie advises using the following two-step technique.[3]

Step 1: Identify a negative thought and immediately repeat it in the past tense. This process allows for a transition between the unwanted thought and the desired outcome.

Example: Negative thought: "I'm so stressed out because of the challenges of marketing on social media." (present problem)

Rephrased in the past tense: "I used to be stressed out because of the challenges of marketing on social media." (past problem)

Step 2: Make a progressive statement that will move you forward and put you into a process. Nathalie believes there is great power in being willing or open to learning or trying something that is causing the negative talk. Flipping the dialogue and

3 "Think Yourself Academy." Nathalie Plamondon-Thomas, 2021, http://thinkyourselfacademy.com/.

repeating the statements that move you forward and closer to your goals will be a game-changer when it comes to growing Split-Second Courage.

Example: "I am willing to learn how to market my business on social media."

"I am in the process of learning new social media marketing techniques."

By the way, did you happen to read the forward to *Split-Second Courage*? If not, now is the time to go back and hear from the amazing Lt. Col. (Ret) Bryan Price, PhD, founder of Top Mental Game, a program of mental preparation for the highest levels of athletes and beyond. On the *Two Fit Crazies and a Microphone* podcast, he shared a fantastic exercise he uses to tame that unruly self-deprecating inner voice.[4]

Bryan used the exercise while coaching a high-ranking Division I women's basketball team in preparation for their season. The process was simple. He asked the girls to tell him what negative things they told themselves when they missed a shot or made a bad play.

Their responses ranged anywhere from a mild, "You suck," to a much more hurtful, "You are the worst f***ing player ever."

4 Christine Conti and Brian Prendergast, "Interview with LTC (Ret) Bryan Price," April 12, 2021, in *Two Fit Crazies and a Microphone*, Episode 220, produced by TFC Productions, podcast, 1:16:29, https://www.twofitcrazies.com/the-podcast/2021/4/12/ltc-ret-bryan-price-phd-founder-of-top-mental-game-director-buccino-leadership-institute-seton-hall-university-episode-220.

Bryan then masterfully turned the tables on them. First, he asked the girls if they would ever talk to their teammates or anyone else like they speak to themselves. Then, to drive the point home, Bryan asked one athlete to direct her response at him yet speak exactly as she does to herself. Reluctantly, she let go with a salvo of the most inappropriate derogatory verbiage.

Heaping insults on someone she respected and wanted to please was embarrassing, especially in front of everyone else. Yet her inner voice did the same to herself all the time.

Your inner voice has no business talking to yourself that way!

You have been sabotaging yourself for years with negative self-talk and self-deprecating expressions, and it is now a habit. So how do you flip the switch? According to Bryan, you can't change this habit overnight. However, you can learn more positive habits to replace negative self-talk.

Practicing positivity helps build confidence, increase focus, and manage emotions for peak performance. To strengthen your positivity, you can use visualization, imagery, and other techniques. These are also crucial for expanding your Split-Second Courage.

My favorite tip is to respond out loud to yourself whenever you start getting negative. For instance, you may be at work, and you forgot to send out that important email. Or you just messed up an invoice, and now payroll is delayed. Immediately, the negative thoughts pop into your head, beginning their litany.

"You are such an idiot."

"You are so stupid."

"There you go again…making another mistake. You will probably get fired."

Instead of internalizing "that voice," argue with it. Yell at it! Tell that voice where to go and then reverse that message! Say it out loud! I guarantee you will feel so much better, and maybe you and the people around you will get a nice laugh out of it as well. Try this!

"I'm not an idiot, nor am I stupid. I am smart, and I am awesome!"

"Oh well, I made a mistake, and I will be more careful in the future. I am a great employee, and I bring a lot to the table!"

"I am not a loser! People love me! I am fun, and I care about my work! I love being me!"

Mindset Over Matter

"Your talent sets the floor, but your mindset sets the ceiling."
—BRYAN PRICE

Twenty-five years ago, I played for one of the top volleyball clubs on the east coast. Two to three times each week, my father served as my personal chauffeur for that ninety-minute trip to and from Queens College amidst unbearable New York City rush-hour traffic. He made sure that I was always early for those two-and-a-half-hour grueling practices where we were being programmed to know nothing else but to win.

Our coaches treated my teammates and me like machines. As I reflect on what we endured during those extreme physical and mental beatdowns, I can hardly believe how more people didn't quit. They told us we were terrible athletes, that we were stupid, that we deserved to be screamed at, and that making a mistake on the court reflected our character. It was upsetting and abusive, but we took it.

During some practices, our coaching staff invited extremely talented athletes to scrimmage our team. Playing tough competition is always a great way to elevate your game, but these practices were humiliating and destructive. On countless occasions, coaches kicked my teammates out of practice sessions or forced us to run until we collapsed or left, tears streaming down our faces. This was the reality for girls who desired to be a part of the most successful club on the East Coast.

These coaches' methods to program "winners" are similar to those deployed by drill sergeants at a military boot camp. While I do not agree with these methods used as an athletic coaching style, I do understand the reasoning. Mental toughness stems from overcoming intense obstacles that wear down both the body and the mind. As Jenny's story of being locked in a closet shows, mental and/or physical beatdowns and abuse don't have to diminish you. You can transform these experiences into valuable tools to develop your Split-Second Courage. Your worst moments in life can become your biggest assets if you learn to shift your mindset.

But as a seventeen-year-old athlete, I hadn't signed up for boot camp, and I didn't understand. I thought my coaches were the spawns of Satan. I didn't realize this was the way they understood how to coach our mindset. They yelled and screamed until we became resigned; they pushed us to the point of physical exhaustion until we became stronger; they refused to let us quit. They instilled in us the tools we needed to be resilient in the face of any opponent we would come to face. This was my first experience with mindset coaching and its effectiveness.

So, though I was not a big fan of this coaching style at the time, it had a greater effect on me than I realized. In fact, becoming immune to the negativity and berating of my coaching staff was a skill that proved most useful throughout my journey as I learned to harness my own Split-Second Courage. Whether you are a businessperson dealing with unhappy clients, a teacher dealing with disgruntled parents or administrators, or a parent dealing with your hormonal and angry teenagers, the ability to control your emotions and reactions in adversity is a valuable tool. Most people have to learn the ability to stop taking others' words personally and just deal with the situation; it doesn't just come naturally. I had the opportunity to learn it early, thanks to the very coaches I once thought were so unfair or out to get me.

Take some time to reflect on the moments when your life had mentally or physically beaten you down, when you hit rock bottom, or when you didn't think that you could go on. How did you feel? How long did the feeling last? When did you realize you were going to get back up? When was your "yes you can" moment? How did you start to climb out of the dark place?

These experiences are your greatest assets.

Nature vs. Nurture

> ***"In each of us, two natures are at war—the good and the evil. All our lives, the fight goes on between them, and one of them must conquer. But in our own hands lies the power to choose—what we want most to be, we are."***
>
> —ROBERT LOUIS STEVENSON

To this day, whenever I hear an allusion to *Lord of the Flies* by William Golding, I begin to twitch. During my fifteen years teaching high school English, this glorious text (insert sarcasm) was a staple in my sophomore classes. It is about a plane full of English boys who crash on a deserted tropical island and become savages until their rescue. I will not go into all of the devilish events that Golding portrayed in his classic work, but I will point out the perfect illustration of "nature vs. nurture" as it relates to Split-Second Courage.

Nurture

Golding's characters were adolescent British boys raised in upper-middle-class households and educated in boarding school. Exposed to societal norms, they seemed to understand and value ethics, rules, family, education, money, power, praise, and punishment. When they arrived on the island, they knew only a life of order, schedules, and discipline. They chose a leader, divided up responsibilities, and believed in the power of the conch, the shell they designated as a symbol reflecting unity, order, and civilization.

Nature

As weeks progressed on the seemingly tropical paradise, the once-civilized boys gradually abandoned all rules, becoming wild, blood-thirsty, hedonistic savages. They sought the adrenaline that accompanied a rewarding pig hunt, they desired the satisfaction that came with devouring a big meal, and they sought power each time they got into a fight. As their societal restrictions dissolved, they lost their fear and gained the ability to act with courage.

Nurture Your Nature

I'm not advocating totally abandoning all rules and running wild. But people need balance. For many people, trying to follow all the rules all the time leads to stagnation and a lack of achievement. Being "good" isn't always about perfectly following the rules anyway.

You may have been conditioned by society on how to act, what to say, and even what to think. Your upbringing may have greatly shaped your views on vocation, religion, or gender identity. Yet the real "you" is in there, and so is your Split-Second Courage. It can free you from the constraints that have prevented you from learning and experiencing so much about yourself and the world around you. It is time to let go of your rigid, non-authentic "nurture" and begin living your real, free "nature."

In theory, this sounds wonderful! "I'll just forget about societal rules and be me! I'll wear my underwear on the outside of my clothes, make garbage snow angels in my living room, and eat ice cream for breakfast!" Right?

Not exactly. While quitting your mundane job, telling your boss to "kiss off," moving to Bali, and letting your children fend for themselves might happen in your dreams, this is not what I mean by nurturing your nature.

By definition, "human nature" is a bundle of characteristics, including ways of thinking, feeling, and acting, that humans naturally possess. Thus, people often regard the term as capturing the essence of humanity as a collective.

To understand your "nature," take a deep dive into what you believe to be your code of ethics, morals, and values, and ask yourself more about them. What do you truly value? Why? What does it mean to you? Why?

Now: What actions, activities, or routines do you keep in your life that may not align with what you believe—and if they don't align, why are you doing them?

On the other hand, what types of things do you *wish* you were doing in your life that you don't ever seem to get to do? Why aren't you doing them?

Nurturing your nature requires you to be a bit selfish. It also requires that the people you associate with understand that this is who you are, and you find these things fulfilling, even if they don't agree. They're not you. As long as you aren't harming anyone else, why does it matter?

In fact, having the right people around you makes a huge difference in nurturing your Split-Second Courage. Aside from your immediate family members, who are the five people you spend the most time with each week? Are they friends? Co-workers? Family members? How do they live their lives? Do they nurture their nature, or are they stuck in life because of too much "nurture"? Are they happy in their career choices or current jobs? Do they often engage in activities that make them happy, such as going on vacations, attending parties, going to the movies, exercising, or simply laughing? Or do they often complain about everything and everyone? (By the way, if you can't identify anyone around you who constantly complains, ask yourself, is it me?)

If they are "stuck" and unhappy, yet they disapprove of the changes you want to make, they aren't very credible. They definitely aren't good role models or support networks for Split-Second Courage, and you're better off finding others who are more open-minded and accepting of your goals.

By nature, humans have a competitive and hedonistic side, but they suppress that side of their true nature for many reasons—fears of rejection or judgment, fear of failure, or even fear of success. They try to define themselves by others' definitions of "good" and then attempt to fit in this narrow mold. That's why not everyone makes it up the corporate ladder, comes out of the closet, quits that unfulfilling job, or even attempts to reveal their "inner rock star" no matter how much they fervently wish to. Secretly, they actually fear the very things they want. Before you take any tangible actions, you must practice nurturing your nature—not being afraid of it.

As I mentioned, to grow Split-Second Courage, you must first identify what makes you happy and accept your true nature. It doesn't matter what it is. Whether you have always dreamed of going back to school for your PhD, getting that promotion at work, spending more time with your family, or driving that black Range Rover with the titanium rims and smoked-out windows, it's time to unapologetically accept that this is what you want. Get up every single day and remind yourself who you are and what you want, and go get it.

Survival of the Fittest

"To be the best, you must be able to handle the worst."
—ANONYMOUS

After talking with former New York City firefighter and decorated endurance athlete Matthew Long, I will never again use the saying, "I feel like I just got hit by a bus." That's because Matt actually knows what it feels like to get hit by a bus.

In one of the best Brooklyn accents you will ever hear, Matthew told me one of the most unforgettable stories of tragedy, triumph, and strength that I will ever hear.

Just at dawn one December morning in 2005, Matt carefully navigated the New York City streets, which were not yet jam-packed with their weekday rush-hour commuters. He was heading to the firehouse to meet his buddies for an early-morning swim session to prepare for their next endurance event. Already addicted to the mental and physical challenges of marathons, triathlons, and of course, the IRONMAN, Matt had taken the lead in training his fellow firefighters a few days each week. They would meet early each morning to train and have breakfast, and then they would head back to the firehouse.

That particular morning, Matt never saw the four-ton charter bus before it pinned him in the ten inches of space between its chassis and the pavement. He and his bike became one as the bike's steel frame split his torso in half, ripping his abdomen open. Blood gushed from his femoral artery as his life literally came to a screeching halt.

Within minutes, police nearby pulled Matt's mangled body from the wreckage and used their bare hands to apply pressure to stop the massive blood loss. Once Matt arrived at the nearest hospital, doctors and nurses performed one surgery after another, frantically attempting to save what little life he still had left.

Even after fifteen years, Matt vividly recalls the story his mother later told him about that fateful day.

"The doctors told her that I had a 1 percent chance of surviving," he said. "The amount of blood loss was just too much, but my heart was still beating—at an extremely low rate. My mom turned to the doctors and told them that they needed to keep going because I would be running the Boston Marathon that spring."[5]

---

5 Christine Conti and Brian Prendergast, "Matt Long: Athlete/Survivor/Speaker," April 23, 2019, in *Two Fit Crazies and a Microphone*, Episode 99, produced by TFC Productions, podcast, 1:18:38, https://www.twofitcrazies.com/the-podcast/2019/4/23/matt-long-athletesurvivorspeaker-episode-99.

Afterward, throughout two of his most physically and emotionally challenging years, Matt not only recovered from what should have been a fatal accident but also went on to complete multiple marathons, triathlons, and IRONMAN races and set some world rowing records. He did what was supposed to be impossible—he beat the odds due to his arsenal of Split-Second Courage.

Although the accident took no more than a split second, Matt's regular physical and mental training had unknowingly been preparing him for this moment his whole life. He had been prepping his heart, his lungs, and the muscles throughout his entire body to endure the massive stress and trauma that took place on that horrific day. The physical and mental fatigue he put himself through while training and competing in races, as well as the knowledge he had learned from crossing so many finish lines, came together to create his secrets to surviving the horrific accident. Matt possessed the perfect juxtaposition of strength and resiliency—and the nature of a fighter—that he needed not only to survive but to thrive. When it comes to Darwin's theory of natural selection, or "survival of the fittest," Matt Long certainly proves the hypothesis.

While Matt's case is an extreme one, the point is not that you need to start preparing in case you ever get hit by a bus. You can't prepare for every possible potential event. The true point, however, is that while you may or may not have control over what happens in a split second, you can certainly have some control over what happens next and how your body and mind will react to that event. If you are in general prepared mentally, physically, and emotionally for the challenges your life will bring you, you will be far more likely to not only make it through them but to learn how to use them to become a tougher, more seasoned fighter. You will be able to bounce back from events that might overwhelm someone else. And once you understand the depth of your own fighting spirit, your fear will fade, and your courage will strengthen.

Reflection: Split-Second Science

1. What are three positive things that your Personal Assistant reminds you about each day?
2. What are the three things that your Personal Assistant says to you to try to sabotage your life?
3. What qualities does your ideal internal Personal Assistant have? Why haven't you "hired" this person yet?
4. Identify one negative thought and immediately turn it into the past tense. Write it down! Now carry a small notebook or use your phone notes app to write all of them down for a day. The number and content may surprise you—just think how that has affected you every day through your life.
5. What are five things you wish you could do—no matter how trivial they seem—that you haven't? Why not?
6. What are five things you do every day that don't reflect your true core values?
7. What does "stop living your nurture and start living your nature" mean to you?
8. What is holding you back from your "nature?"
9. If you experience major trauma, are you in the mental and physical shape to survive it? Why or why not?

CHAPTER 5

The Path to Split-Second Courage

Exercise the 'SSC Muscles'

"If you want to run faster, run faster."
—BRIAN PRENDERGAST

I'D LIKE TO THINK THAT IT IS PRETTY OBVIOUS. If you want to get better at anything, including your Split-Second Courage, you must practice. Now, unless you are someone like the famous NBA basketball player Allen Iverson, who is notoriously known for his blatant disregard for practice, you understand that you will need to put in some hard work.

"We're sitting in here…talking about practice. I mean, listen, we're talking about practice, not a game, not a game, not a game, we talkin' about practice," Iverson said.[6]

6 Matt Walks, "The Little-Known Story Behind Allen Iverson's 'Practice' Rant," *ESPN*, May 7, 2021, https://www.espn.com/nba/story/_/id/29143112/the-little-known-story-allen-iverson-practice-rant.

And just for the record, even Allen Iverson really did know the value of practice. It turns out that this quote was taken out of context after he skipped out on practice due to the death of a loved one.

Doing the work means the difference between sitting around dreaming of living a more fulfilling life or actually doing it. You can either jealously read others' social media posts about their latest adventures, exciting career changes, or decisions to sell their houses and move to their dream locations, or you can be one of them, posting your own interesting news. Which do you want to do?

As I've mentioned, Split-Second Courage doesn't happen overnight. I don't expect you to immediately pick up the phone to book your first skydiving experience after finishing this book (although I speak from experience that skydiving is pretty awesome). Nor would I expect you to go compete in a triathlon after a single twenty-minute practice jog around the block. Instead, I'm asking that you start making small changes to exercise and build your SSC Muscles, just as you'd start doing to prepare for a triathlon.

To do this, you need to take a deep dive into your "why" to figure out your "how." Use this list below as a practice guide.

- ☑ How would increasing your Split-Second Courage change your life?
- ☑ Why do you believe this?
- ☑ What small decisions can you make in the next week or month that may require additional Split-Second Courage?
- ☑ Are you armed with the tools to cope with the decisions that you make?

- ☑ What are the worst- and best-case scenarios that will occur from this decision?
- ☑ Are you okay with them? Why or why not?

Rethink Your Relationship with Time

"The bad news is time flies. The good news is you're the pilot."
—MICHAEL ALTSHULER

I came across a man named Jesse Itzler about five years ago. His name kept popping up on some of my social media threads, and his adventurous lifestyle captivated me. At the time, he was known to rent entire mountains in Vermont and hold insane running races. He also invited hundreds of people to one of his homes to run up and down a steep hill on his property as many times as possible. This was known as "Hell on a Hill." He also released two books: *Living with a Seal,* in which he chronicled his experiences moving a Navy SEAL into his New York City apartment with his family, and *Living with the Monks,* detailing a few months he spent living in a secluded monastery learning the ways of the sacred monks.

Jesse, a fellow Long Islander, also happens to be the man behind the theme song for the New York Knicks, is a former rapper, founded the Marquis Jets (sold to Warren Buffet), created ZICA Coconut Water (sold to Coke), and is the spouse of the self-made billionaire and SPANKS creator, Sara Blakely. Due to their great success, Jesse and his wife could easily buy an island, sip cocktails, get massages, and live the rest of their lives in peace and tranquility. However,

Jesse doesn't believe in being comfortable. He believes that living a happy and fulfilling life requires constantly putting yourself in uncomfortable situations and experiences where you may fail.

One technique that Jesse preaches is his ability to rethink and reimagine his relationship with time. In many of his keynote speeches and coaching workshops, Jesse discusses his personal relationship with his aging parents. According to Jesse, thinking about time with regard to the number of times you see your friends and loved ones may significantly improve your ability to act with Split-Second Courage because you more clearly understand what you have to gain or lose.[7]

For example, suppose your parents are eighty years old and will live to the age of eighty-five. If you see them twice a year, there is a chance you may only see your parents ten more times in your lifetime. If you are fifty years old and have two kids in high school, you may only have two to three more years living together before you are empty-nesters and entering the next stage in life. Those are years of a specific time in your relationship with your family that you will never get back in the same way again.

The ability to rethink your relationship with time is a powerful tool for acting and coping with decisions that may at first seem frightening and unrealistic. Are you a planner? Do you plan every minute of your day, week, month, or year? Do you ever deviate from your plans? What happens when things don't go as planned? What happens when a really cool opportunity opens up? Do you ever just "go with the flow," or does doing that make you anxious?

---

7 Jesse Itzler, "Top 10 Rules," June 20, 2018. Video, 29:54. https://youtu.be/a3xzrY1pUt4.

Understanding how you process change will lay the groundwork for growing your Split-Second Courage in all aspects of your life.

Let's take a moment and think about how many invitations or events you have declined in the last few years. If you can, go back even further and think about the last five to ten years. Why was it that you declined to attend that work party? Why did you pass on showing up at that barbecue? Birthday party? Wedding? Weekend getaway? Job interview? Date? What held you back from saying "yes"?

If you are to change your behavior and your relationship with time, let's start here! Ask yourself, "If I don't attend this event and I were never to see these people again, am I cool with that?" The answer may surprise you. What frightens you more? Is it entering a new and uncomfortable environment, or is it never taking chances to encounter new experiences? Now, because life is finite, we can insert the relationship of time into this equation. Sit back, review your past decisions, and think about what your life could have been like. What did you miss? What if you had been in the room instead? What could be different now?

Jesse's concept of time fueled his Split-Second Courage to overcome every obstacle, no matter how daunting and unattainable it looked. He could rationalize why it was important to act in any given situation because, in his perspective, it could be his only chance to do it.

As with anything I've said, keep in mind a sense of balance. Please understand that I am not telling you to go out and have a "year of yes"; I am here to remind you that just one "yes" could change your life. Learning to identify the most important "yes" moments becomes as crucial as attaining the courage to be in them.

If you get the chance, listen to Jesse Itzler talk about this and more on episode 100 of the *Two Fit Crazies and a Microphone* podcast.[8]

"What would life be like if we had no courage to attempt anything?
—VINCENT VAN GOGH

Nothing Like 'the Present'

Let's get one thing straight: To grow your Split-Second Courage, you must reimagine your "present." As you begin to reflect on your relationship with "the present," be sure to think about what it means to be present.

Contrary to what you hear on social media, humans cannot multitask effectively. We can absolutely handle various tasks placed before us in succession, but our brains can only process so many things at one time. Did you know that the National Transportation Safety Board (NTSB) reports that "drivers engaging in visual-manual tasks, such as dialing or texting, increases the risk of a crash by three times"? You can't effectively attend to two things at once.[9]

When you're carrying around the past or future while dealing with the present, you're basically doing the equivalent of multitasking. You're not able to be fully in the present because you're focused on the past, and you're not able to be in the past because

---

8 Christine Conti and Brian Prendergast, "Jesse Itzler—Entrepreneur/Author/Endurance Athlete—Building Life's Resume," May 1, 2019, in Two Fit Crazies and a Microphone, Episode 100, produced by TFC Productions, podcast, 43:40, https://www.twofitcrazies.com/the-podcast/tag/Jesse+Itzler.

9 "Eliminate Distraction in Transportation," National Transportation Safety Board, accessed October 7th, 2021, https://www.ntsb.gov/Advocacy/mwl/Pages/mwl3_2014.aspx.

it's gone. Unless you have a time machine, you're not going to get it back.

How can you focus on making more courageous decisions in life and fully embrace or cope with the stressors that accompany them if you don't have a laser-focused mindset in the current moment? The answer is simple. You can't!

To improve your Split-Second Courage, being able to recognize and move away from your past is crucial. Have you made mistakes in your past? Have you done things that you are not proud to admit? All of us have done things in our lives that we're not proud of—things such as lying, fighting, cheating, stealing, or more. Sometimes it's difficult to forgive ourselves for past mistakes. Personally, it took me decades to forgive myself for the way that I treated others in some situations or how I reacted in ways that I am not proud of. However, I've learned that realizing that you cannot change the past is the first step toward becoming more present.

Past mistakes are one of the main reasons we don't give ourselves permission to try new things in the present. They stack up like proof that we shouldn't do all of these other things that we want to do. Our pessimistic inner assistant loves them! "You can't do X. Remember that time you tried to do something like that? How did that turn out? Terrible! And what about that other time? Terrible, too! What makes you think you should do anything like that again? Ha!"

You can listen to the negating inner assistant, or you can turn it back on itself.

"Yes, I have made past mistakes. I do remember that one time. But boy, did I learn some good stuff there! That's why I would do it differently this time—I could probably make a great plan now!" All your inner assistant does is bring up your fears. Learn to counter them with facts, information, logic, and understanding.

In addition, when allowing yourself to detach from the past, it is imperative to stay away from overly anticipating and worrying about the future. This is easier said than done, but being present requires complete focus on the experience at hand and the ability to fully embrace the current moment. The simple act of stopping to see, smell, listen to, or hold onto something and appreciate it for a few short seconds each day is a great start.

The time is now. Parts of your past are still with you now, but they've changed as you have. Take a moment and really look at that fun family picture hanging on your wall. You rush by it each morning but fail to see it. Think about the event. Relish how you felt there and how much you cherish the people you were with.

While it may seem cliché, bend down and smell three different roses the next time you walk by that rose bush. Crank up that song that sets your soul on fire on the radio. It reminds you of being carefree and ready to conquer the world when you were sixteen. And what about taking a few seconds to hold or hug your spouse, your children, your pet, or even yourself each morning and night? Our minds are so cluttered with trivial lists, items, worries, and agendas that we forget what it is like to be alive.

The Gift

Picture it: You are eight years old, in your childhood home. It is Christmas morning, or Hanukkah eve, or Festivus for the rest of us. You have tried to be on your best behavior, hoping that all your "goodness" has not gone unnoticed throughout the year. And what to your wondering eyes should appear, but a bounty of shiny presents, big and small, wrapped in beautiful paper with gigantic bows strewn here and there.

You reach down and gently flip over a gold tag, and it reveals YOUR name! You flip over another. Yet again, it's YOUR name! Now you flip another, then another, then another. They all have YOUR name!

Feverishly, you tear open the first gift of this unbelievable treasure, and it contains EXACTLY WHAT YOU WANTED! You are overflowing with happiness; you feel elated, excited, energized, and grateful. You are feeling all those good feelings! This experience is AMAZING!

Without hesitation, you pick up the next present and shred its wrappings. It is also EXACTLY WHAT YOU EVER WANTED! Now onto the third, fourth, fifth, and sixth. These were all EXACTLY WHAT YOU WANTED! You are on top of the world!

Still on cloud nine, you reach down a snatch up that seventh package. Effortlessly ripping through the shiny paper and quickly opening that brown box, you are ready for the next best thing that is coming into your life. For why wouldn't all your presents be glorious? You have always followed the rules (more or less); you have worked hard; you have sacrificed; you have always tried to be a good person.

However, as this present reveals its contents, you realize that THIS gift was never on your list. This gift is completely wrong. This gift must be a mistake. "Why would someone give me THIS gift?" you ask, your ardor fading.

This gift can't possibly be for you...but there is no way to give it back. Whether you like it or not, this gift is yours, too.

You begin to feel anger, disappointment, sadness, fear, and hopelessness. But what do you do? You have options, right?

1. You can continue to feel bad for yourself.
2. You can think logically and try to find out why you received this.
3. You can create ways to use this gift.

If you are like me, you have "opened a lot of presents" in your life. Some of those have been exactly what you wanted—true love, a wedding, the birth of a child, the job of your dreams, decades of health, and peace of mind due to financial security.

However, some of the "presents" life has awarded us have turned out to be things we wouldn't wish on our worst enemies. These may have consisted of abuse, addiction, betrayal, depression, death, grief, hurt, pain, loss, and disease. These are the presents that will try to break you. They will rock you to your core. They will bring you to your knees and even cause you to doubt every decision you have ever made in life. You will sit at the end of your bed and weep. You will feel alone. You may even turn your back on your faith and question your existence.

However, the ability to hit rock bottom, to allow yourself to "feel all the feels" yet keep moving forward, will prove to be one of the greatest gifts to nurture your Split-Second Courage.

While the great Winston Churchill states: "If you are going through hell, keep going," I would add that those of us who have been through hell and made it out alive possess more strength and Split-Second Courage than we could ever imagine. Then the challenge becomes finding a way to tap into this hidden magic to make more courageous and insurmountable changes to other parts of our lives.

In all honesty, I did not start really living until I got sick. My illness was my hell. Yet, it's also true that at the age of thirty, opening the "gift" of an advanced autoimmune disease eventually proved to be one of the best things that ever happened to me. At the time of my diagnosis, I thought my life was over, but it was just beginning.

Remember Grandma Jeanne, my role model for my initial despair? After enduring an initial six months of darkness and self-exploration, I began to recall childhood memories of Grandma Jeanne that made me realize I had done her a disservice.

Although a quadriplegic, she had one of the most positive mindsets I have ever encountered. She was a lighthouse, a symbol of hope, and a gift to all who crossed her path. While her body failed her, her zest for life and her ability to inspire others through her electric personality was truly magical. Her gift was her crippling disease. It gave her the ability to inspire the world to keep fighting and see life as a miracle.

As a child, I did not understand the magnitude of her pain and suffering, but I did understand the joy and gratitude she brought to her family and friends. Even towards the end of her life, any room always got a little bit brighter and the smiles grew just a little bit wider when Grandma Jeanne was wheeled in. In hindsight, I know that she fully embraced her "present," and that was how she was able to move past any pain, anger, fear, and depression and be courageous in the face of disease...which brings me to the story of El Correcaminos.

El Correcaminos

El Correcaminos is the Spanish word for "roadrunner." However, it also happens to be the name of an amazing father-son running duo by the name of Hiram and Angel Cruz. The first time I set my eyes on Hiram, he was steadily pushing his teenage son, Angel, in a shiny red Team Hoyt racing wheelchair towards the finish line with great determination. It was beautiful.

It is hard to describe Hiram's transparent love for his son, who was born with severe disabilities. Since birth, Angel has been diagnosed with cerebral palsy, epilepsy, dysgraphia, global development delay, sensorineural deafness, and the list goes on. "Some days, Angel is very calm, while other days, he may be extremely hyperactive," Hiram reflects. However, the one act that brings them both great joy and allows them to spend valuable time together is running races.

El Correcaminos has completed over fifteen half-marathons and over ten marathons, with Hiram pushing his beloved son, Angel, a present like no other. So, what does this have to do with growing Split-Second Courage, you might ask? The answer is sometimes difficult to see when it comes to human suffering or the diagnosis of life-altering disease. Hiram chose to see Angel's diseases not as problems but as the gift of a great opportunity to build a powerful relationship with his son through an activity that he genuinely enjoyed, running.

El Correcaminos also pushes Angel to raise awareness for Easter Seals, Children's Hospitals, and therapeutic organizations for the disabled around the world. Angel's life—what others might see as a terrible misfortune—serves as a useful example of how important it is to value all life's "presents."

Before you make your next decision, ask yourself what kind of joy it will bring and how it will positively or negatively affect the people you most care for. Channel your inner "El Correcaminos."

If you have confidence in the projected result, then pull the trigger and make that courageous decision. However, if you cannot imagine how your relationships will improve or expand from the decision, then it should be off the table.

> *"Success is not final; failure is not fatal:*
> *it is the courage to continue that counts."*
> —Winston Churchill

The SSC '10-Count'

For a decade, I was addicted to a television show called *Lost.* I am not ashamed of my obsession. On the contrary, I genuinely believe it strengthened my marriage, improved my relationships with co-workers, and also provided many supplemental resources for my seemingly dry high-school English curriculum.

The series' premise revolves around a motley group of passengers who have survived a catastrophic plane crash that left them lost on a deserted tropical island, far from civilization. As the series unfolds, each character reveals whether or not they are equipped with Split-Second Courage when faced with life-or-death decisions.

In the pilot episode of *Lost,* more specifically the exact scene immediately following the catastrophic plane crash, Jack and Kate, two of the main characters, reveal my inspiration for the SSC "10-Count."

Far removed from the plane wreckage strewn across the once pristine beach, Jack, a spinal surgeon, and Kate, who is later revealed to be a fugitive, take a moment alone to regroup.

Still in disbelief about their situation, Kate says something to Jack along the lines of, "You don't seem afraid at all. I don't understand."

Jack's answer is the perfect example of how to grow and nurture Split-Second Courage.

"Fear is sort of an odd thing...When I was in residency, my first solo procedure was a spinal surgery on a sixteen-year-old kid, a girl." He explained that at the end, after a thirteen-hour procedure, he accidentally ripped the girl's dural sac, the part of the spinal cord where all the nerves come together. "That membrane is the thinnest tissue, and so it ripped open, and the nerves just spilled out of her like angel hair pasta," he said. "Spinal fluid flowing out of her...I was terrified. It was just so crazy, so real...so I just made a choice. I'd let the fear in and let it take over, let it do its thing, but only for five seconds. That's all I was going to give it. So, I started to count: one...two...three...four...five...And it was gone. I went back to work, sewed her up, and she was fine."[10]

While you may not have survived a plane crash or performed a thirteen-hour spinal surgery, you've probably had moments when you were terrified beyond words. I would also bet that you have faced situations where you had to make a tough decision, even call upon what you now know as your Split-Second Courage. What went on in your mind? What tools did you call upon to make that decision to act, run, or do nothing at all? While Jack counts down from five, the SSC 10-Count is similar but starts from ten. It is one of the most powerful tools to help you face and overcome fear.

Use the SSC 10 Count before you finalize your decisions and choose to act. In real-life situations, the 10-Count will help you avoid saying those words you can never take back. It will allow

10 *Lost*, season 1, episode 1, "The Pilot: Part 1," directed by J.J. Abrams, Bad Robot, Touchstone Television, ABC Studios, aired September 22, 2004.

you time to formulate your thoughts and think through a "game plan." It will help you speak the words you always wanted to say, quit that unfulfilling job, or end that abusive relationship and go out and be the person you always dreamed of being.

Embracing your greatest fears and deciding that "yes you can" accept the obstacle before you may also lead you to experience higher highs and greater joys in all areas of your life. The key is that the 10-Count allows you the vital experience of feeling all the feels, but only for a short time. They don't get to master or overcome you. They don't get to prevent you from acting.

The 'Extended' 10-Count: Heather's Story

I first connected with Heather after she reached out to me over Facebook Messenger with some questions regarding personal training. She was an extremely successful and independent woman who had recently been through a hellish year in the field of healthcare. Heather had spent the last twelve months holding cell phones up to the ears of dying residents as they breathed in their last breaths, connecting one last time with their socially distanced family members across the United States. It was apparent that she was a woman of strength.

I agreed to take on Heather as a client a few times each week to help her jump-start her fitness routine after a year of putting her own health and fitness routines on hold to care for others. In addition, Heather informed me that in a few short months, she would not only celebrate her fiftieth birthday but also celebrate a huge milestone in her battle against breast cancer.

As I got to know Heather, she shared with me powerful stories of her personal struggle: the moment when she received a grave diagnosis, the stress she underwent traveling to countless doctors' visits, the pain of chemotherapy, the difficulty continuing her full-time job, the decision to go forward with a double mastectomy, and the physical and mental healing process that ensued.

"How did you remain so resilient and strong throughout such a traumatic time?" I asked one evening.

Without hesitation, Heather replied, "I decided that I would only have cancer on Fridays. That was the day I would let it in, and then it could not have any more of my time."

She explained that, immediately after her diagnosis, she was devastated. Depressed and defeated, she felt her cancer was defining her. However, Heather knew that to have any chance of beating the disease, she needed to find a way not only to accept the cancer and honor her feelings but also to continue to live as normally as possible. That is when Heather decided cancer could have Friday, but the rest of the week was for herself.

This mindset was similar to the 10-Count, but for a long-term situation that required mental fortitude and perseverance. Throughout her treatment, Heather scheduled all her doctor's appointments and other procedures on Fridays. She allowed herself to cry as much as she needed on Fridays. She allowed herself to feel pain, anger, and resentment, but only on Fridays. She granted herself permission to feel all these things until the stroke of midnight on Friday. Then on Saturday, she could remind herself that she had once again made it through another day of beating cancer. Every Friday until the end of her long journey towards victory and recovery, Heather faced and overcame her greatest fears. Friday after Friday, she endured her "10-Count," and Saturday after Saturday, she realized she had once again overcome some of her greatest fears.

While the 10-Count may work when faced with smaller obstacles, Heather needed to stretch out this concept over the course of a specific, repeated day so that she could complete her full ordeal. Her ability to let in all the "feels" and accept a cancer diagnosis, but only on her terms, put her in the driver's seat when it came to controlling a seemingly uncontrollable situation. In fact, a very courageous Heather is about to celebrate another year cancer-free, and her Split-Second Courage and resilient mindset continue to grow!

Split-Second Courage comes in many forms. Harnessing it may allow some people to simply step outside their comfort zones and speak up for themselves at work; however, for others, it may allow them to react, cope, and overcome situations that feel overwhelming. Though Heather's solution is not technically a split-second decision, it uses the same mastery of time that will allow her to take control of her mind and emotions while remaining in the moment. By developing this discipline, you also develop the mindset that enables actual Split-Second Courage within the moment as well.

"Courage is resistance to fear, mastery of fear—
not absence of fear."
—MARK TWAIN

Reflection: The Path to Split-Second Courage

1. What is your relationship with time? Think about relationships, family, traveling, work responsibilities, eating, exercising, etc. Do you feel you have enough time for these things?
2. Using Jesse's concept of time, how many more times will you see your parents, grandparents, siblings, and good friends if you live until you are eighty-five years old?
3. What are some of the BEST "gifts" of life experiences you have received?
4. What are some of the WORST of these types of gifts that you have received?
5. What are at least two positive things you can take away from the "bad" gift?
6. Why do you believe you have been blessed with these "gifts"?
7. Have you ever used the 10-Count or taken a few breaths to muster up courage before making a tough decision?
8. What times in your life did you need more than just a 10-Count to let in and "feel all the feels?"
9. What parts of your life could use a 10-Count?
10. How do you plan to implement the SSC 10-Count into your daily life to grow your Split-Second Courage?

CHAPTER 6

The Platonic Conception

Visualize and Conceptualize

"So we beat on, boats against the current,
borne back ceaselessly into the past."
—F. SCOTT FITZGERALD, THE GREAT GATSBY

EVERYONE WHO KNOWS ME knows my obsession with F. Scott Fitzgerald and his most famous novel, *The Great Gatsby.* I fell in love with the story as a teenager and eventually wrote my undergraduate honors thesis on the relationship between Fitzgerald and his characters. I went on to teach American Literature for over a decade and discovered a powerful tool necessary to foster Split-Second Courage. Jay Gatsby, the main character of the novel, reveals how to successfully create a "Platonic conception of yourself" in order to live a more fulfilling life.

For those of you who are not familiar with the book, Jay Gatsby is a fictitious character based on actual people who lived on the affluent north shore of Long Island, New York, during the Roaring Twenties.

Gatsby, whose birth name was James Gatz, spent the early part of his life as a poor boy who enlisted in the army. He eventually fell madly in love with a rich girl, Daisy. Since "poor boys don't marry rich girls," James Gatz was obviously out of his league—but he had a plan. He would create a "Platonic conception" of himself and become the man he dreamed of being. This new man would be a man of wealth and power, a man of celebrity status, a man of mystery and romance, but most importantly, a gentleman worthy of winning the heart of his Daisy.

It didn't matter that he came from nothing because James was going to be something. His goal clear, his eyes laser-focused, and his actions speaking volumes, James Gatz made every decision with the strategy of positioning himself just a little bit more squarely within his Platonic conception. Every conversation he had, every book he read, every relationship he fostered, every business transaction he made, every piece of clothing he bought, and even every car and house he acquired became part of his premeditated transformation into Jay Gatsby. This was the man he would show off to the world, and most importantly, the world would believe it.

Unfortunately for Gatsby, the transformation led to tragedy. The upper society he worked so hard to fit into turned out to be shallow and superficial. Daisy, as part of that society, also turned out to be unworthy of Gatsby's selfless devotion. Was his sacrifice a mistake he should never have made? Maybe, or maybe not. Maybe it was a lesson he needed to learn, and the experience was worth it. Whatever the case, he had the courage to make the decision. In the end, his decision led to a series of events that eventually caused his death, and he did not win the woman of his dreams. Daisy was unable to understand the true depth of his love for her or his courage, as she lacked the capacity for either.

Would Gatsby say his choice was still worth it? Probably. He made the decision, and he was willing to own the outcome.

Gatsby took the Platonic conception to an extreme. Most of us will never change our names, engage in criminal behaviors, or completely disown our pasts—yet we all can recreate ourselves to be the person of our dreams. We don't have to make the mistakes Gatsby did. It's possible to be wise yet still demonstrate Split-Second Courage. In fact, wisdom is just another tool that can help you let go of your fears rather than feed them.

You Know More Than You Think You Do

Now, you may have a million reservations about the notion of creating a Platonic conception, especially after what it meant for Gatsby. You may have even just come up with more excuses for why doing something like that is not possible. However, most people have more practice than they might think with this valuable Split-Second Courage tool. You'll know I'm right when I ask you to take a walk down memory lane and think about what this word conjures up in your mind: HALLOWEEN.

That's right. The crazy holiday when you get to become whomever you wish to be. What an amazing opportunity we had to explore some Platonic conceptions of ourselves. For one chaotic day, you morph into your wildest dreams! Babies become devils, grandmas become astronauts, dads are superheroes, and every teenage girl becomes some sort of "woman of the night." This was one of my favorite terms used by my mother when I tried to leave the house in what we call a "slutty outfit." (In hindsight, she was always right. I shudder to think about some of the ensembles I put together back in the day.) But I digress. Let's get back to the concept of Halloween. Some of us really went all out on this. For weeks, months, or sometimes even years in advance, we would plan our costumes with great care. For some, tons of research went into ordering the perfect clothing and buying or creating appropriate props, tools, or fake weapons. Then, there was the time that went into rehearsing that new accent, mannerism, or behavior required to complete the transformation. It took planning; it took time; but it was exciting. It may have even caused some anxiety, but the result was well worth the wait.

You spent so much time preparing and anxiously awaiting "that day" when you would embrace this new persona. It was finally here, and you were ready and confident! You would sweep into the Halloween party or head out to the candy-filled streets, smiling proudly at every gasp of amazement over your costume.

When it comes to developing your Split-Second Courage, think about the process you went through to become that superhero, villain, fireman, or rock star on Halloween. I am sure it went something like this:

1. Who do I want to be? Why?
2. What do I love, admire, or wish to emulate about them?
3. What do they look like? What do they wear or carry?
4. How do they act? What are their mannerisms?
5. Do they have an accent? Specific dialect?
6. While you may not be preparing to transform into a wild

and crazy monster, or so I hope, these are the exact same questions you must ask in preparation to create your Platonic conception. For example, if you are hesitant and fearful to take the plunge and be that entrepreneur you always dreamt of, the time is now. You already have the experience—now let us put it into practice.

Take out a pen and a piece of paper and write down your answers to the following questions:

1. Who or what do I secretly admire and wish I could be or be like? (This could be an actual person or a character from a book, TV show, or movie.) Why?
2. What do I love about this NEW persona?
3. What does this NEW persona look and feel like?
4. How does this NEW persona act, and who are their friends, confidants, and business acquaintances?
5. How does your NEW persona speak/communicate with others?
6. What about becoming this new persona worries me—and why? (You need to know this for a reason—stay tuned.)
7. How can becoming this new persona change my life for the better?

Becoming an IRONMAN

In the fall of 2017, I was contacted by *Health Monitor Magazine*, a worldwide publication that sits in every doctor's office in the United States and beyond. Maybe it was divine intervention, but after learning that I had rheumatoid arthritis and was advocating exercise, movement, and holistic approaches to fight autoimmune disease on my platforms, the magazine's editor reached out to me. To make a long story short, I not only appeared on the cover, but they also featured me in a two-page interview with the hopes of inspiring other RA fighters like myself.

A few months after the magazine launched, I received a very surprising email from the IRONMAN Foundation. They heard about my story and invited me to compete in IRONMAN Lake Placid, New York, in July of 2019 on their behalf. At that very moment, I stopped breathing for a few seconds.

Of course, this is also when my own inner Personal Assistant decided to step in with its "helpful comments."

"Oh, my God, Christine! What did you get yourself into? An IRONMAN? You can't do that! You are not a strong swimmer, you have never been on a tri-bike (nor do you know what that is), and you have never run a full marathon on tired legs. What were you thinking? You could never do this! You are not the collegiate athlete you once were. You are old. You have kids. You have a disease."

Can you relate to this?

Just like that, I was scared to death. I let that damn voice speak to me and instill the most overwhelming fear and doubt that I had worked so hard to overcome in the decades prior.

But I didn't have the time or inclination to listen to it. I had seven short months to become a proficient open-water swimmer and figure out how to function in a constricting wetsuit. I had seven short months not only to come up with the money to purchase a bike but also to learn how to ride it competitively. (In all honesty, I still do not completely understand what a tri-bike really is.) And, I had seven short months to figure out how to train for such a momentous race. Hiring an expensive coach was out of the question since I had resigned from the steady paychecks and healthcare benefits of a full-time teaching career.

I had seven months to create and implement my Platonic conception.

I had seven months to become an IRONMAN.

I would be lying if I told you that it was easy to transform into an IRONMAN. The process unfolded like this.

Over the course of those seven months, I used what I call my "WHY/ACT" plan. Each day, I wrote down the action I took to move just a little closer to my goal and the reason behind it, or why. While I prefer writing on a calendar because it provides me a certain satisfaction when I can check off lists, this is some of my "WHY/ACT."

WHY	ACT
Track every workout	Get calendar and pen
Improve hydration	Eat more fruits and veggies
Body repair/Mood/Energy	Get 7.5 hours of sleep (no excuses)
Flexibility/Injury prevention	Yoga/Rolling/Stretch every day
Ease anxiety	Interact with IRONMAN groups
Purchase tri-bike	Search used bikes/Borrow?

I could write down every detail of this list, but the most important thing is for you to realize the key, which is to break your big goal into smaller sub-goals you need to achieve (these become your "WHY" list), and then use small actions (your "ACT" list) to achieve each of them. This process moves you closer to your Platonic conception each day, week, year.

Throughout those seven months, I planned my transformation as if I were getting ready for Halloween. I analyzed clothing, learned applicable skills, implemented new behaviors, learned new IRONMAN language, and even changed my food choices. Little by little, transforming myself became less daunting and more exciting with each passing day.

I also started writing notes to myself to shut up my Personal Assistant and keep her from spewing more self-deprecating words when I least expected it. Emblazoned on my desk calendar and my phone, these messages read, "Is what you are doing moving you closer to achieving your dreams?" I always made sure my answer was "yes." This meant I was making progress in becoming my Platonic conception and growing my capacity for Split-Second Courage.

This process does not happen overnight. In fact, contrary to the message delivered in the well-known book *The Secret*, you do not just think about increasing your capacity for Split-Second Courage without a solid action plan. It takes time. It takes persistence. And it must be broken down into small digestible steps. Again: Decisions may only take a split second, but consistently making more courageous decisions in a split second takes time and work.

The 'Impostor'

Here's another way to think about the Platonic conception: My kids play this mind-numbing multiplayer survival video game called "IMPOSTOR." The game takes place deep within a laboratory, where someone is up to no good. That someone is YOU!

Your goal in the game is to create as much mayhem as possible. Players attack their co-workers, sneak through vents, and sabotage various types of equipment. According to the directions, the goal is "to bring this entire place to its knees" by moving fast. For example, if your co-workers can clean up the mess you made and fix all the equipment you broke, all before you cause more damage, then you lose. I know, it sounds magical!

The reason I bring up this or any video game that uses avatars is the fact that they allow us to be impostors. Remember the character you created for Halloween? That was an avatar. Have you ever created a character to play in a video game? That was an avatar, too. What about when you put on your best pants suit and transformed into a confident negotiator for a work presentation? Or put on a puppet show for your children? In all of those cases, you used avatars. You became an impostor. Own it!

The word "impostor" has developed a negative connotation through the years. It is defined as "a person who pretends to be someone else in order to deceive others, especially for fraudulent gain."[11] However, the Online Etymology Dictionary says that its meaning once was more neutral: "one who passes himself off as another."[12] It is an important tool to harness to further grow Split-Second Courage. For example, have you ever taken on the roles or responsibilities of your co-workers, family members, or friends when necessary?

While I am sure you will not be surprised, I have lots of "impostor" experience.

---

11 Oxford UK Dictionary, s.v. "Impostor," 2021. LEXICO, accessed at https://www.lexico.com/definition/impostor.

12 Online Etymology Dictionary, s.v. "Impostor," accessed August 12, 2021, https://www.etymonline.com/search?q=impostor

The first time I really remember being an impostor, I was in high school, working as the "assistant to the assistant" of the mayor of Babylon, New York. I was a pretty big deal (insert sarcasm). However, when the "real" assistant would go on her lunch break, I moved my butt into her chair, rearranged everything on her desk, and answered the phone as "the assistant." Honestly, I remember granting people the authority to do things like possibly cutting down a tree and emptying a pool into a drain. I also discussed their personal problems in conversations that went completely beyond my job description, but for that hour, I was "The Impostor," and it was thrilling.

Although that is just one of my more innocent impostor roles, impersonating someone—even the person you plan to be—is a skill, and like any other skill, it must be responsibly practiced and nurtured. The more comfortable you can become walking in someone else's shoes, the more you will understand their circumstances and be able to show empathy. You'll increase your confidence and success in impersonating greatness—because you will understand it.

So instead of seeing an impostor in a negative light, start to remember that even the most successful people have "faked it until they made it" and "done it until they became it" at one point or another. If you need some examples, just Google the backstory of Andrew Carnegie, Steve Jobs, Oprah Winfrey, and Richard Branson, just to name a few. Society deems these people mavericks, game-changers, innovative thinkers, and pioneers in their own right, but they were all impostors at one point. They saw the life they wished for themselves, created their Platonic conception, and became an impostor. Until they fully transformed into the powerful influencers and thought leaders they will be remembered as, little by little, they were impersonating those who they admired, those who came before them, and oftentimes those they wished to surpass.

Channel Your Inner Drag Queen

My obsession with drag queens began in my early twenties. For a short time, I lived in a shoebox of an apartment in the East Village in New York City, the home of some of the most beautiful and unavailable men in the world.

Those daily walks around Astor Place, and even the occasional longer treks to Chelsea, soon became to me like a drug. All I saw were gorgeous men smiling, holding hands, and gossiping, all with impeccable fashion sense and perfectly placed hair and nails.

However, at night, many of these same men took on a vastly different identity. Every evening like clockwork, nearby at Lucky Cheng's Drag Cabaret, these men morphed into the most stunning women you will ever see. They donned sequined dresses, displayed their flawless long legs, showed off their perfectly styled hair and makeup, and set themselves free! They had moxie; they had confidence; but most importantly, they fearlessly gave themselves permission to be bold and authentic!

Drag queens will always serve as an impeccable example for those seeking to grow their Split-Second Courage. They acknowledge who they most identify with, allow themselves to embrace their feelings when dressed in drag, and unapologetically let the world see them as they see themselves. Standing there shining bright for all to see, they represent the refusal to follow societal norms in pursuit of happiness.

Obviously, you don't have to become a drag queen to be more courageous. They're just an example of the process to find the "new you," the one who will surprise you and challenge you to grow in a different direction—but also one you're happier moving in. You might have to be the impostor—but only until you are comfortable in your "new skin."

Being an impostor means that you are an outlier—you act, but most of all, you understand the power of harnessing Split-Second Courage to improve your life. How did your mentors and role models face and triumph over adversity? This will give you an idea of how to emulate them for similar success, until one day you find—maybe even to your surprise—that you've become one of them.

Take Action

The journey to create and implement your Platonic conception requires planning, hard work, and patience. To grow your capacity for Split-Second Courage and become more comfortable taking risks and setting off on adventures, you must start at the very beginning.

Who do you desire to be in life?

You have embraced your "Halloween persona" for decades. Why not try a different version of that now?

What could possibly go wrong?

Okay. Now: What kinds of answers to that last question did your negative inner assistant just fill your mind with?

That question—and those answers— hold us back from creating and implementing our Platonic conceptions of ourselves for a lifetime. Here are some of my favorites:

"Don't be ridiculous. You'd be a laughingstock."

"Oh, brother. No one could really do that in real life."

"Why do you want to make a fool of yourself? What if So-and-So finds out how silly you are and wants nothing more to do with you?"

And so on.

Don't you find it interesting that you have no problem taking the time and effort to transform yourself for one day each year, but you lack the courage and patience to follow through on doing it for the rest of your life?

I'll bet that in your child's mind, it wasn't overwhelming, anxiety-ridden, or anything to lose sleep over, right? If you did lose sleep, it was probably because you were too excited about it to sleep.

It's time to let your inner kid have some free rein again. Focus on the potential positive and exciting experiences you could be missing, and convince yourself that the time is NOW!

Now, think about how this NEW persona handles your current life.

If you are unhappy in your job, what can your NEW persona do *right this moment* to get the wheels in motion for a possible change in career, a new degree, or even an advancement? Make a list! Then set weekly and monthly goals to do these things. Sharpen your vision of the future—buy that sketchbook and draw a picture of who you will become and how your life will be more fulfilling. Hang that picture at your desk. Carry it with you wherever you go. Refer to your list or your drawing every time you feel unmotivated or lack courage, and use it as fuel to light your fire!

To overcome your state of fear or inability to take action, start by doing one little thing—it doesn't matter what, or even if it's just imaginary to start. Speak up just once this week at a meeting—or if you're not ready to do that, just think about what you'd say and how you'd say it. Just once, give the advice you have been holding onto. Just once, think about how you will feel if you continue to never do anything about the thing that's bothering you—and think about how you *can* do something about it.

Remember how you wrote down the things that worry you about your new persona? Those are fears of being yourself. You're going to need to overcome those, too. That's why I had you write them down— because unless you bring them up in a list and are willing to argue with them, you're never going to talk your inner assistant out of bringing them up all the time. It's time to take charge and manage your assistant instead of letting your assistant manage you.

It's time to find your Split-Second Courage.

Reflection: The Platonic Conception

1. What was your favorite Halloween costume? What did you "nail" about this character? What do you think failed?
2. Other than on Halloween, have you ever been an "impostor"? If so, what were the circumstances? How did you feel? Was it a challenge? If you've never been an "impostor," why not?
3. What decisions would you make differently as an impostor? Work? Family? Leisure? What characteristics would you change about yourself?
4. What is holding you back from taking action or impersonating greatness?

5. How could impersonating others help you take action to start working towards your goals?
6. What is one goal you want to achieve? What values does it reflect/Why is it important to you?
7. What does the Platonic conception of yourself—who can and will achieve this goal—look like? What characteristics does this person possess that you feel you lack? How will he/she help you achieve your goal?
8. Begin to visualize your NEW persona to help you reach your goals. How does this person live each day? What does he/she like to do best? What kinds of friends does he/she spend the most time with?
9. Make a list of all the "things" that your NEW persona will act upon.
10. Keep a journal about how this conception of yourself feels after taking action.
11. How has your life changed after acting? Think about your career, relationships, income, and more. What are they like now?

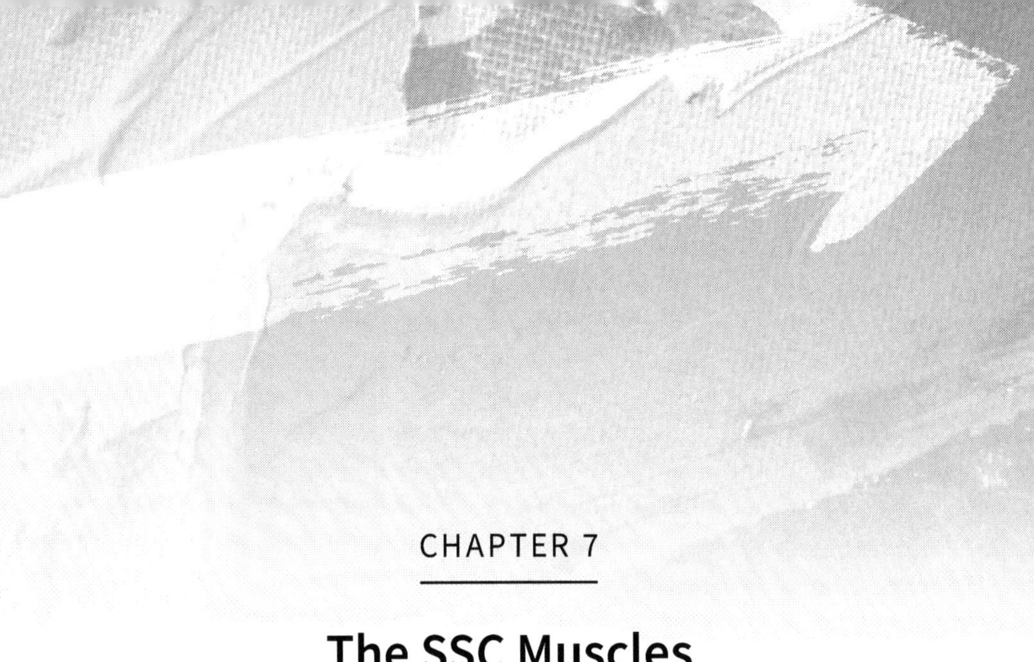

CHAPTER 7

The SSC Muscles

"Courage is like a muscle. You strengthen it with use."
—RUTH GORDAN

The Facts!

"What you do speaks so loudly that I cannot hear what you say."
—RALPH WALDO EMERSON

HOW MANY TIMES HAVE YOU BACKED DOWN because you lacked the courage to act or speak up even though you knew you were right? Take a moment to consider why your "Split-Second Courage Meter" was stuck on zero. Were you afraid of the consequences of being right? Of being wrong?

Now ask yourself this: Why were you not afraid of the lasting consequences of inaction?

What you do speaks volumes!

Early in my career, I had the pleasure of teaching a lovely "cherub" (insert sarcasm) I will refer to as "Jesse" to protect his identity. Midway through the spring semester, Jesse transferred to the high school where I taught junior English. All the administration told me was that I would be getting a new student who was very bright. Over the following decade as an educator, I came to learn that when parents called their children "very bright," it always meant something greatly different.

What it actually meant was that the student was not responsible for his or her learning, and if he or she didn't achieve anything in class, it was the teacher's fault. So, if you're his teacher, and this student doesn't get straight As in your class, it's your fault, and there will be consequences. The parents will blame all their child's problems on your poor teaching skills and lack of classroom management. They will email you and call you daily to tell you how you are failing their son or daughter and will barrage you with a plethora of other personal family matters that make you extremely uncomfortable. Nothing will be off-limits. I'll spare you the sordid details.

On the rare occasions when Jesse chose to grace 6th period English class with his "very bright" presence, he sat in the third seat in the row of desks that butted up to the windows. He always donned a different matching NBA basketball cotton sweatshirt and sweatpants combination, paired with the most expensive and newest Nike basketball sneakers on the market. And just for the record, if you are skeptical about how I am able to recall such minute details, please be advised that a teacher never forgets their first great teaching trauma.

While Jesse owned some extravagant jewelry, I don't think he owned a pen, paper, or book. Attempting to read or write would perhaps have been nearly impossible due to the way he sat slumped in his chair with both feet up on the empty desk in front of him like his personal footrest, one earbud shoved into the ear that faced the window (as if I could not see it), and his right hand inside his sweatpants, moving around as if he were shifting the gears of an expensive sports car.

I know—you probably didn't want to hear that part, but this tells you what I was up against.

Understandably, this behavior traumatized everyone in the class. Unfortunately, however, reporting it to the school nurse or psychologist was useless. In fact, the parents never responded to any of my attempts to contact them—that is, until that one fine day when I was called down to the principal's office. (By the way, whether you are a student or a teacher, you still get that "oh shit" voice in your head and that knot in your stomach.)

As I entered the administrative boardroom, I found myself facing the principal, a vice-principal, the English supervisor, the school counselor, two psychologists, a psychiatrist, Jesse's parents, and my personal favorite—a lawyer dressed in a black suit.

"You are the reason my son is not going to get into Princeton," Jesse's mother shouted at me. "He is an extremely bright boy, and you have ruined everything. He never failed anything before he came here."

And that is how the meeting began.

I was a twenty-four-year-old teacher fresh out of graduate school with very little assertiveness.

Or so I thought.

Armed with documentation of deplorable attendance, spreadsheets of missed assignments, copies of detention slips, and email trails of requests for parent calls and meetings, my Split-Second

Courage had no problem showing up that day. I had the facts, I spoke the truth, and they had no choice but to listen.

They were messing with the wrong girl.

They, on the other hand, had not spoken the truth nor given the full facts. It turned out that Jesse had been kicked out of his previous school for dealing and taking drugs; he currently frequented school only to deal; and the $300 allowance that he received from his neglectful parents each week went to fund his own drug habits. I vindicated myself easily that day. To this day, I still laugh when I think about them telling me I was the reason their son did not get into Princeton.

But, while the previous outlandish claim was unfounded, it highlights an important reminder: Always remain vigilant about knowing and collecting all the facts in any situation. Building an arsenal of courage may require extensive research, the time and willingness to gather and sort through information, and the ability to identify and make cohesive arguments that support your decisions.

Defending yourself, your values, your ethics, and your beliefs requires courage, and that courage will grow if you support it with facts. Facts don't lie. How often do "the facts" affect the decisions you make in your life? If you're not clear about the facts, you won't know whether you're acting on the correct impulse, which may make you hesitate.

Strengthen Your Permission

"Kid, you'll move mountains! Today is your day!
Your mountain is waiting. So get on your way!"

—DR. SEUSS, *OH, THE PLACES YOU'LL GO*

As a child, do you remember reading Dr. Seuss? From *Oh, the Places You'll Go* to *Green Eggs and Ham* to *The Lorax*, his writing not only draws readers into fantastical worlds of fun but also relays powerful life skills and advice. Dr. Seuss empowered children to seek their dreams, overcome obstacles, try strange new things, and even stand up for what they believed to be right and just. Then, through the years of formal education, teachers reiterate these words, serving as guides and mentors to enhance their students' ability to carry out Dr. Suess's advice. They help their students increase their cognitive skills and instill in them a love for learning. The educational process drills reasoning skills, logical thinking, communication skills, and historical facts into students' brains, preparing them to face and overcome the obstacles ahead.

So, the question is quite simple: When did you shut down Dr. Suess's and other inspirational voices in your head? At what moment did you choose to close the doors of new opportunities? When did you turn your reasoning skills against your dreams, convincing yourself that you no longer had permission to do the things that gave you a sense of satisfaction, fulfillment, or joy? When did you stop "taking that chance" or "going those places" and start believing that it was too late to chase after the life you always imagined?

What happened?

When did you no longer care about granting yourself permission to be strong and hold fast to your dreams?

From an early age, were you convinced that money was the root of all happiness? Were you, like me, brainwashed into believing that studying hard and playing by the rules would get you a good job, the opportunity to earn lots of money, and the ability to live "the good life"?

Were you told, as I was, that selflessness was a trait that every adult, especially women, must embrace if they wished to please their spouse, be a good parent, and experience success?

Did you know that all these pieces of supposedly "good advice" could not be farther from the truth?

In reality, there are no hard and fast "rules" to play by.

In life, you have the choice to be a martyr or a model. ALWAYS BE THE MODEL!

Take that chance!

Follow your gut!

Go after your dreams!

Yes, you can!

However, if you don't feel you deserve something, all the positive affirmations in the world will not help you attain it. You just won't give yourself the key ingredient that leads to Split-Second Courage: permission.

So, it's time to get to work and reflect on why you feel as though you should accept being relegated only to doing things that dim your shine and cause you to suffer. Did you grow up with the idea that to be "happy" and experience success, you must go without what you personally define as actual happiness? Is that true "success"? When did we become resigned and accepting of someone else's mundane, cookie-cutter idea of how we should be?

Think back to your childhood. Did your religious upbringing teach you that you were required to sacrifice some of the things you wanted in life to find eternal happiness? In school, did you suffer through classes like chemistry even though you had no interest because that is what you were told to do? Did your parents, teachers, coaches, mentors, and society all assure you that only through sacrifice will you get into that prestigious school, get hired by that well-paying company, and then be able to say, "I've made it"?

It is about time you give yourself the permission to be disruptive and challenge the existing dogmas. While skipping out on a chemistry class may not have been an option, think about what you are NOT giving yourself permission to do or to enjoy in life right this very moment. How would your life change if you allowed yourself to go out with your friends once a month, if you told the office that you would no longer take calls after 5:30 p.m., or if you told your family and friends what you really desired to be in life?

Granting yourself permission to strengthen your "Split-Second Courage Muscles" will allow you to embrace and celebrate what you desire in life. It will not only set you free but also grant permission to those around you to strengthen their ability to practice making more courageous decisions, also.

Well Suited for Transformation

Although it takes time to develop the courage to grant yourself the permission to make monumental or life-altering decisions, as I've mentioned, you can start small and build your skills slowly. Just one decision can be the catalyst to change the course of your life.

For example, you never know how something like a white pants suit could possibly have such an enormous impact on your life.

It was the summer of 2000 when I was interning for Morgan Stanley Dean Witter at 1585 Broadway in New York City. If you are unfamiliar with this building, it is one of the massive skyscrapers that surround Times Square and is best known for its hypnotizing ticker incessantly scrolling the most up-to-date stock market data. However, this was also the summer when I had my first run-in with the white pants suit.

On occasion, my friend Ari and I would sneak away from our desks during our lunch hour and head toward the Avenue of the Americas to check out the latest fashion trends. Ducking in and out of department stores with a laser focus on catching a great deal, we always made it back to work just in time to stash any recent purchases under our desks without being missed. However, things changed the day I first set eyes on the white pants suit.

I will never forget walking into that department store and being overcome by the vision of myself walking into a meeting wearing that powerful white pants suit. I could picture it clearly. My co-workers would be discussing their latest projects and reviewing spreadsheets, but when I walked into the room with my powerful white pants suit, everyone would stop. The attention would be on me. People would want to know my opinion and hear my thoughts about future stocks and investments. I would have arrived!

So, what did I do? I walked right over to that white pants suit, picked it up, began heading to the cash register, and finally flipped over the tag. I stopped in my tracks. What was I thinking? I was an intern in my early twenties living in New York City. I couldn't afford that $200 white pants suit. This would be an irresponsible purchase, and I would NOT give myself permission to buy it even though I knew it would bring me such joy, such a sense of empowerment, and maybe even a permanent job offer.

Fast forward twenty-two years. I am still talking about that damn white pants suit. While it may seem trivial, the fact that I denied myself the permission to buy the white pants suit continues to serve as a valuable reminder to make sure you allow yourself the ability to experience joy, love, and maybe even make more courageous decisions every once in a while. While you may or may not love an awesome white pants suit, I urge you to think about what "white pants suit moments" you may have in your life.

If something brings you joy, you'll need very little Split-Second Courage to make that decision—it should be quick and easy. Your inner assistant has no qualms about it!

"I love that restaurant. Of course, I will go."

"That person brings me happiness. I will spend more time with them when I can."

"I just got a bonus at work. I can't wait to buy those shoes I have been eyeing for months."

However, when the decision holds higher stakes that may take you out of your comfort zone, or if it requires a longer commitment or lacks immediate gratification, it will naturally require you to turn up the meter—in other words, raise your level of courage. Will it pass the "permission" test?

To answer that, let's go back to the NEW you—the persona you have created, which you're transforming into. This is the new boss. Your inner assistant is still set up to serve the needs of the OLD boss. Maybe he or she needs some help understanding that that person is not there anymore. As the NEW boss, you're going to have to explain to your inner assistant what's what now. You need to instill in your assistant your vision, goals, and plan for achieving them.

Your assistant is used to being your "protector," and the intention is good, but it's coming from your former goals—safety and protection from the unknown (in other words, protection from fear).

The NEW boss doesn't worry about the things the OLD boss did. Fear is not an obstacle now. So instead of letting the inner assistant trip you up with fear, put him/her to the task of identifying the potential obstacles *and ways to get over them*. Your inner assistant is already adept at identifying all the obstacles or reasons why you can't do something—why not put that to work for yourself?

The next time he/she questions you, question back. Maybe he/she can help you identify holes in your thinking—but maybe you can identify holes in theirs. Your inner assistant will give you great practice at putting together your facts and your arguments.

"You can't do that!"

"Why not?"

"Well, because you don't have the money to do that."

"How much money do I need?"

"You'll need at least X amount of money."

"Are you sure? I could eliminate A and B expenses and still do it. See? I've already worked out all these facts here. Do you see any concerns with these numbers?"

You also need to make your inner assistant aware that you are taking responsibility for the consequences of your decision and that you are willing to take the risk. Eventually, you won't allow your inner assistant to keep you from doing what you want to. Even if it brings up something you haven't thought through, that just tells you that you need more facts, not that you shouldn't pursue the goal.

Essentially, the goal is to say to yourself, "How am I going to handle the consequences of this decision?" instead of, "Should I make this decision that brings with it some unknowns?" This is the real challenge when it comes to strengthening that Split-Second Courage Muscle.

So, what can you do? Start incrementally.

1. Each day, make one small decision that brings you joy. It can be ordering from your favorite coffee shop or restaurant or indulging in your favorite Netflix show.
2. Each day, make one small decision that takes you out of your comfort zone, whatever it might be. Try a new restaurant. Introduce yourself to someone you don't know. Turn off all electronics and talk to your spouse or family members for fifteen minutes.
3. Track your progress. You'll be surprised at how much you have changed. Write yourself a note about the different things you've done/tried each day, week, month, or year.
4. Look at your progress and challenge yourself to go bigger. Do things you have always wanted to do! Each day, try something that makes you just a little more uncomfortable than yesterday. Go to that new restaurant—this time by yourself. Join a new group where you don't know anyone. Make a family date to do something you've never done that will take everyone out of their comfort zone—paintball, a theatre production, or an adventure hike. Take a bigger risk each week and see how it pays off.
5. Repeat 1–4 infinitely.

Seek (the Right) Help

Also, I realize that though this is not rocket science, for many, including myself, strengthening the Split-Second Courage Muscles requires some extrinsic help. Have you ever asked someone to open that lid that would not come off, unscrew that pesky wine cork, or help assemble that twenty-thousand-piece kids' tricycle at 1:00 a.m. on Christmas Eve after you have had a few glasses of wine? Just this week, my daughter zipped up the back of my dress before a meeting, and my husband zipped up the back of my wetsuit before an ocean swim. My guess is that you have asked for help before and that you have received it!

When it comes to strengthening your Split-Second Courage Muscles, finding the right people to help is paramount. So, who are the right people?

They're the ones who just "get it." They understand what you're trying to do, and they share your passion and want to help.

I remember like it was yesterday. My lungs felt as if they were able to take in more oxygen than usual, the sun was shining, and the last box was finally loaded into the back of my Jeep. I had dreamt about this moment for years, and it was finally coming true.

"Goodbye, high school! Goodbye, stuffy classroom! Goodbye, ridiculous curriculum that hinders curiosity!"

I had already taken a sabbatical for a year, but I had no plans to return because I believe that "looking back f***s with your neck." In addition, I had no plans of not "making it." Sure, I left a great salary, medical benefits for my family, and a pension. Most of my family and friends thought I was crazy or having a nervous breakdown. However, I had a plan to ensure that I had help turning up what I now call my "Split-Second Courage Meter" when the doubt and self-deprecating talk entered my head.

For years, I had met the most amazing people from all over the world. From my travels presenting at fitness and physical education conventions to coaching volleyball teams, running marathons, and my involvement with the local chamber of commerce, I knew a lot of people. The problem, however, was that I was working so much that I never had the time to get to know these brilliant entrepreneurial people who were out there chasing their dreams. That was about to change. The week after I resigned, I created a list. Little did I know that this list would significantly change the course of my life.

It was a warm July afternoon when I walked into Brian's cozy office, where he coached his clients on their health. Locally recognized for his incredibly fast speed as a runner, Brian was surprisingly calm and laid back compared to what I was expecting. In the next hour and a half, we shared running stories, spoke about our passion for helping others find joy and fun through movement and nutrition, and most importantly, decided that we could help change more lives if we were to collaborate in some way. That afternoon, Brian would give me something that I needed more than anything—the permission to strengthen my Split-Second Courage by supporting my crazy idea to start our own worldwide platform.

It wasn't a complicated conversation. It went something like this.

"Hey, Brian. I think we should start a podcast," I said.

Without hesitation, he replied, "I'm in."

And that was it.

He just got it.

It didn't stop with Brian, either. One by one, I reached out to every person that fascinated me. I wanted to talk with those who were making great changes in the world, the people who had overcome intense adversity and triumphed even when the odds were stacked against them. The people I met would eventually become my "wolf pack" and show me how to grant myself permission to find more of my Split-Second Courage. These are the people whose stories fill the pages of this book, so their legacy can live on.

Reflection: The SSC Muscles

1. How strong do you think your SSC Muscles are, based on a scale of 1 (poor) to 10 (strong)?
2. What is ONE thing you can do each day to strengthen those muscles? Remember to start small.
3. Name three instances in your life where you showed courage in the moment. How did it feel to be courageous? Did anyone notice?
4. How well do you recall facts about your past experiences? Does your memory ever fail you or play tricks on you when attempting to recall exact instances?
5. Are you willing to keep a "fact journal" about impending or past decisions and what steps you took to arrive at a decision?
6. Do you consider yourself a martyr or a model?
7. Do you have a "white pants suit" story that haunts you? Why? What did you learn from this?
8. Who are the five people you surround yourself with the most? Do their attitudes help to strengthen or weaken your SSC Muscles?

CHAPTER 8

The Manufacturing Process

The SSC Immune System

Don't take life too seriously. No one makes it out alive."
—ELBERT HUBBARD

BEFORE I TELL YOU ABOUT HOW TO manufacture Split-Second Courage, I want to take a minute to tell you what might get in the way: The psychological immune system.

As a serial learner and podcast junkie, I stumbled upon the most fascinating TED talk while attempting to distract myself from the incessant bumper-to-bumper Belt Parkway traffic on the south shore of Long Island. Headed to my mother's house for a quick visit, I pulled up the long queue of talks that I had yet to find the time for, and one particular topic caught my eye. A man by the name of Dan Gilbert gave a talk in 2004 that was titled

"The Surprising Science of Happiness."[13] I was intrigued by what "science" he would reveal since the ability to grow Split-Second Courage is directly related to one's ability to move away from fear and gravitate towards happiness.

Gilbert began his talk by explaining his fascination with the evolution of the human brain. In fact, he revealed that since the time when our early ancestors roamed the earth, humans have developed a frontal lobe, specifically, the prefrontal cortex. This is an extremely powerful tool that is responsible for one's ability to simulate experiences. In short, this means that we now have the ability to project the outcome of various situations, predict the effects of future decisions, and create mental simulations of our lives based on our current situations and prior experiences. Humans are the only species that can do this.

This ability, in fact, is a crucial part of the human "psychological immune system," according to Gilbert and fellow researcher Timothy Wilson.

Most of us have learned that the immune system is the bodily system that protects us from foreign substances, cells, and tissues by producing an immune response to destroy them. Without delving too deeply into the exact science behind the immune system, the major players are the organs, lymph nodes, lymphocytes, and antibodies.

However, Gilbert and Wilson have theorized that another immune system is also at play—the "psychological immune system."

---

13 Dan Gilbert, "The Surprising Science of Happiness," TED, February 2004, https://www.ted.com/talks/dan_gilbert_the_surprising_science_of_happiness.

While a functioning bodily immune system attacks and wards off foreign invaders and disease-causing agents such as viruses and bacteria, our psychological immune system wards off negativity by helping us to make decisions that will protect our best interests—or so we think.

The "psychological immune system" is a shorthand term Gilbert and Wilson created to encompass several biases and cognitive mechanisms that protect a person from experiencing extreme negative emotions.[14]

People achieve this protection by ignoring, transforming, or constructing information, making the existing situation more bearable while decreasing the appeal of the alternatives. As with the body's immune system, which operates without our awareness much of the time, the psychological immune system operates largely or entirely outside conscious awareness. This is one reason psychologists Gilbert and Wilson coined the term to describe it.[15]

The psychological immune system includes:

- Ego defense, or the tendency to have defensive reactions in any situation
- Rationalization, or convincing yourself your decision is the right one
- Self-serving attribution, or the need to make decisions based on hedonistic needs

---

14 Gilbert, 2004.

15 Gilbert, 2004.

- Self-deception, or the ability to convince yourself you did the right thing, although it was against your ethics or values
- Terror management, or the ability to handle fear
- Fading affect bias, or a bias in which the emotion associated with unpleasant memories fades more quickly than the emotion associated with positive events

So, you ask, how does this relate to growing my Split-Second Courage?

Your psychological immune system might be preventing your Split-Second Courage from showing up—and you may have no idea what's going on!

Leaping to the Worst-Case Scenario

Have you ever thought about why you make or do not make those split-second decisions? The psychological immune system acts without conscious awareness, so people often fail to anticipate its effects. This is one reason people don't do well at forecasting how they will feel in potential future situations. They typically overestimate the degree to which negative events will affect them.

Here's an example of how the psychological immune system influences thought.

How often do you imagine the worst-case scenario before you act? How many times have you been sitting on the runway preparing for takeoff and imagining how you are going to react to that imaginary emergency water landing?

What will I do first?

Will I try to grab my cell phone?

Was that half-sleeping man with the red mohawk and earbuds sitting in the emergency exit row really listening to the flight attendant's instructions about how to open the emergency exit?

Will my seat cushion actually float, or is the airline industry lying to us?

The horrible images and questions swirl through your mind as you feel the panic rise. Why does this happen?

The psychological immune system is trying to protect you. Yet this attempt at protection contains several major flaws.

The Hazard of Impact Bias

One of the reasons we jump to worst-case scenarios in our ability to simulate experiences is due to something called "impact bias." An impact bias is our mind's tendency to overexaggerate the emotional effects of the things that will potentially happen to us or the obstacles we will experience.[16]

Part of the psychological immune system's response is based on these "emotional predictions," which help identify what to avoid.

How many times have you imagined a scenario like this?

1. If my presentation does not go as planned, I am sure I will be fired.
2. If I get fired, I will never find another job because no one is hiring.

---

16 James Clear, "How to Be Happy When Everything Goes Wrong," blog entry, accessed September 29, 2021, https://jamesclear.com/impact-bias.

3. If I don't get hired, I will not have enough money to pay the rent, and I will get evicted.
4. If I get evicted, I will have to live in a van down by the river. (Thank you, Chris Farley, for that timeless reference.[17])

If you often overestimate the extent of a negative event's impact, then you are most likely struggling with an overactive psychological immune system and impact bias. Now, don't get me wrong here; making calculated decisions by predicting events is an important skill. However, it can backfire when it protects you to the extent that it begins to limit your life and affect your ability to experience happiness and fulfillment.

Another problem is that the emotional prediction tends to focus within extremes of fear or anticipation, but in truth, the actual effect can be much smaller.

Remember all those times your inner assistant reminded you of how embarrassed you'll be? How painful your life will be? How terrible everything will be if you did X?

That's impact bias.

Yet how often is your inner Personal Assistant really right? In reality, people often surprise themselves in unexpected situations, and their predictions of themselves and others prove totally wrong.

It's interesting to note that while impact bias overexaggerates negative emotional ramifications, it also overexaggerates predictions of positive emotions such as happiness.

---

17 *Saturday Night Live*, "Matt Foley: Van Down by the River," season 18, episode 19, clip accessed September 29, 2021, at https://www.nbc.com/saturday-night-live/video/matt-foley-van-down-by-the-river/3505931.

From past experiences, we believe we can predict all sorts of outcomes. For instance, we can predict that winning the lottery would provide much more happiness and joy than experiencing an accident and becoming a paraplegic. Based on "wisdom," we can project that we should not quit that safe, financially secure, yet boring and unfulfilling job and follow our dreams of becoming an entrepreneur. Because we have a prefrontal lobe, we can also be sure to never register for that marathon we project that we cannot finish. Just not entering at all is a much better option than entering with a high possibility of failing, right?

Wrong!

The truth is that people who win the lottery overinflate the emotional outcome too—they might be happy at first, but their happiness is no more guaranteed than anyone else's.[18] Happiness is actually a little more complex than that, and it doesn't rely on only one thing happening or not.

The reason is that emotional prediction only focuses in a very fragmented way, narrowing in on one thing as if your life revolves around only it. For instance, if your Personal Assistant calls up examples for you about being "devastated and miserable all the time about not having any money" once you leave your current lucrative job, it is negating the fact that you can make money in many other ways, not only from that current job. Not to mention the fact that having money is nice for paying bills and maintaining your home, but it doesn't automatically confer happiness.

---

18 P. Brickman, D. Coates, & R. Janoff-Bulman, "Lottery Winners and Accident Victims: Is Happiness Relative?" August 1978, *Journal of Personality and Social Psychology, 36*(8), 917–927, https://doi.org/10.1037//0022-3514.36.8.917.

So, if your impact bias can be predicting the wrong things, how will you know if you don't challenge it?

Combating the Negative Psychological Immune System

If you recognize some of these doom-and-gloom tendencies in yourself (or your Personal Assistant!), here are some turnkey methods to improve your forecasting skills.

1. **Revisit the Facts**
   "I remember when Susie's presentation went very poorly, and she was reprimanded by our boss—but she was not demoted or fired."

2. **Be Open to Change**
   "I may not find another job with this company or in this area, but there are plenty of other companies out there that could use my experience and skill set. The world is a big place!"

3. **Talk About It**
   "I am stressed about money and bills, but am I aware of my current finances? How long could I afford to be out of work? Do I have money saved for a "rainy day" that I could access? Do I have family or friends that would loan me money or help me out if I simply asked?" The answer may surprise you!

4. **Play the Odds**
   "How many people do I know who are motivated, determined, and hard-working, who live in a van down by the river?" (Personally, I don't know any, but feel free to prove me wrong.)

If you surround yourself with a positive tribe of people, they will come to your side and support you, just as you would do for them. But if you are thinking to yourself, "I don't know any positive, uplifting people," then it's time for some serious self-reflection. Like-minded people tend to stick together. If you tend to be poor at affective forecasting, are you surrounding yourself with others who also imagine the absolute worst-case scenarios before making decisions? Look around and ask yourself, "Am I attracting negativity?" The old saying "birds of a feather flock together" is true. Did you ever think that maybe you yourself are an energy vampire amongst your co-workers, family, and so-called friends? If so, it's time to change that.

Make Up Your Damn Mind

Your mindset is crucial when it comes to manufacturing your own Split-Second Courage. Ask yourself some questions.

1) How often do you believe things in the format of "This is always the case"? For instance, "When someone has X happen, they will, of course, feel/encounter Y and Z for the rest of their lives." This is a fallacy. When you encounter an obstacle, your ability to manufacture synthetic Split-Second Courage will determine whether you can deal with it or will be devastated by it. You get to decide. Remember, my Grandma Jeanne was confined to a wheelchair for the last few decades of her life but was one of the happiest, most positive people I have yet to meet. Why is that? She decided to be happy.

2) How often do you believe there are always options? Grandma Jeanne did not have a choice when it came to her handicap, but she did have a choice to embrace her current situation and make the most of whatever joy and happiness surrounded her. Jeanne may have only had one choice about her handicap, but

she had myriad choices about how to live her life around and despite it. Those who face devastating traumas or tough decisions in life don't always realize these other choices exist.

3) Do you invest in life? This fascinating concept is expressed in a study that I read about that was done at Harvard University with a group of art students. Their teacher gave everyone in the class a camera and directed them to walk around campus and take a dozen or more pictures of things that held meaning to them. When they returned, they then learned how to develop their pictures by hand in a darkroom. After investing the time to learn the development process, they showed an increased pride in their work. Then, the instructor asked the students to decide on their two favorite pictures. They would get to keep one and give the other to the university archives.

However, the instructors did something interesting: They divided the class in half. The first half had to decide immediately which picture they would keep for themselves and which they would give up. The other half, however, had to choose one picture to keep but could swap out their choice up to a week later if they changed their minds.

What is fascinating is that the students who had to make an immediate and definite choice were much happier with the picture they chose to keep than the students who were given a choice with the opportunity to swap it out.

Take a moment and let that sink in. As I have explained before, Split-Second Courage not only requires the ability to act but the *ability to cope with the effects of your actions.* One of the most important skills to use in growing your SSC is your ability to avoid mentally "swapping" situations. Making more finite decisions in your life will force you to accept the reality of the situation to move forward in a (hopefully) positive direction. No more waffling back and forth, listening to your Personal Assistant blowing you a bunch of hot air about all the negative ramifications it *thinks*—but doesn't *know*—you will encounter.

Allowing yourself to deal with the present will also allow you to start seeking and building from the positive effects of any situation. Use your best judgment, make your choice quickly, and remain unwavering in your decision until you achieve your goal.

Reflection: The SSC Manufacturing Process

1. When faced with a decision, do you tend to predict more negative or positive outcomes? Why do you think you do this?
2. Do you believe that you have an intense impact bias? If so, what are some ways you can address it?
3. What is one thing that you've dealt with in your life that you did not have a choice about?
4. How strong do you believe your psychological immune system is when it comes to decision-making? Does it help or suppress you?
5. How often do you forecast the worst-case scenario?
6. How often do the people around you forecast the worst-case scenario?
7. What was the last worst-case scenario that you imagined for yourself before you made a decision? What was the actual outcome of the decision? Did it live up to your forecast?
8. Name one thing you can do to stop yourself from creating future worst-case scenarios and help you make more courageous decisions.

CHAPTER 9

Dare to Fail Greatly

"Only those who dare to fail greatly can ever achieve greatly."
—JOHN F. KENNEDY

So, You Are a Loser

ALEXANDER (NINE YEARS OLD): "Mom, did you win your race?"

ME: "No, sweetheart. I did not win the Boston Marathon today. If I did, our life would be drastically different."

ALEXANDER: "Okay, so you lost? Then you are a loser?"

ME: "Wow! I never really thought about it that way. Yes, I guess I am a loser, but I am really proud of my attempt. Come to think of it, I have lost every marathon I have ever completed, but I will continue to keep trying even if it means I will continue to lose."

I started running marathons ten years ago as part of my bucket list after my diagnosis. It was something that I never imagined that

I could accomplish because it seemed to be only for the fittest and mentally toughest athletes on the planet. Although I was always an athlete, running was not my forté. In fact, I equated running with punishment. If you got in trouble in physical education class, you ran. If you were slacking at a practice, you ran. I still vividly remember being in first grade when the biggest, meanest, grouchiest old scary lunch lady accused me of talking during quiet time. I still remember her name, but I will omit it from this story to save some face. I was forced to walk and jog around big orange cones for the duration of my recess. I remain traumatized to this day.

While I knew very little about the sport of running and often associated it with torture, runners have always fascinated me. How could anyone run for hours—or for 26.2 miles, the distance of a marathon—and live to tell? How could your legs, feet, and hips handle that amount of impact? Would your body just collapse after a certain amount of time? These questions haunted me. So many people around the world willingly signed up, paid good money, and participated in these grueling races year after year. They even seemed to enjoy it!

I began to educate myself. I read books on running, listened to podcasts, sought out the most experienced runners in my community to pick their brains, and I also started running. Day after day, I added running into my daily routine. While I wasn't fast, I was consistent and determined. Over time, I worked my way up from 5k's to half-marathons, eventually completing full 26.2-mile marathons without dying.

However, the point of this story is not to highlight the obvious. Yes, "practice makes perfect" and "consistency is key" are both particularly important lessons, but most importantly, I was actually setting myself up to experience more losses. To this day, I have yet to win any of my races, yet my Split-Second Courage grows, and I feel more fulfilled each time I toe the line at another event.

To sum this up, LOSING IS IMPORTANT!

If you are not winning at every game, event, or job opportunity that comes your way, that's fantastic! In fact, I want you to practice losing, and often! Honing your ability to cope and handle loss of any kind increases Split-Second Courage when it comes to making more high-risk decisions in life. Take a moment and think about how often you lose every day. Remember, losing comes in many forms. Do any of these situations sound familiar?

1. I didn't make it through the light before it turned red.
2. I didn't hear my phone when it rang, and I missed the call.
3. I didn't show up for the meeting because I completely forgot.
4. Dunkin' Donuts didn't have any more chocolate-chip muffins left when I got there.

Winning all the time is impossible, yet we constantly beat ourselves up and engage in negative self-talk or express frustrations when we don't win. If you think about it, almost everyone around you is a loser. For example, when I line up for a running race with a participant pool of more than 50,000 athletes, 49,999 will lose. I often wonder what would happen if I loudly announced to my fellow runners that all of us had little to no chance of winning. While it may not go over too well, it is a fact.

Okay, so the odds may never be completely in your favor. The point here is to practice failure as a means of growing your

Split-Second Courage. I guarantee your life will improve when you start taking more chances and daring to take part in a new experience. These are the things that really matter in life.

So go ahead!

Dare to lose!

Be a loser!

You may enjoy it!

It may just change your life!

The Power of a DNF

Now that you have accepted the fact that you are a loser and have vowed to lose more often, it's time to up the ante. Let's talk about that big scary "F" word that keeps us up at night.

FAILURE!

Since the beginning of time, the mere mention of this word has been preventing people from living out their dreams, daring to take that chance on love, or applying for that new job. That's right, fear of failure is the number one culprit when it comes to your inability to grow Split-Second Courage.

Before you make a decision, do you consider what would happen if you failed? Is failure always an option you leave on the table? If so, I challenge you to erase that option from your brain unless you are ready to have what I call "a love affair with failure."

Let me explain.

I never even knew what the letters "DNF" meant until it happened to me. If you are an endurance athlete, the term can haunt you for the rest of your life. There is nothing worse than seeing a "DID NOT FINISH" next to your name.

Hundreds of big, yellow school busses lined the perimeter of Boston Common as thirty thousand runners from around the world, all wrapped in garbage bags, ponchos, and other assortments of rain gear, huddled together in the forty-mile-per-hour wind gusts and freezing rain. During that forty-five-minute ride to Hopkinton, the home of Athlete Village and the historic starting line for the Boston Marathon, the freezing rain turned to large hailstones, snow, and ice. The already freezing, rain-soaked athletes stared out the fogging bus windows in disbelief.

It was mid-April, but apparently, Mother Nature failed to get the memo that it was spring. Despite what seemed like a scene from the Apocalypse to most runners, this was the Boston Marathon, and there was no turning back. Six years earlier, I made a deal with myself that if I were healthy enough to run and qualify, I would compete. With an advanced autoimmune diagnosis and the cocktail of chemotherapy medications pumping through my veins, I was determined more than ever to inspire others that "Anything is Possible" if you keep that "Yes You Can" mindset.

Athletes spilled out of the yellow school busses and fought wild winds and the strike of icy raindrops as they made a mad dash for the huge white holding area tents at Athlete's Village. The cold was almost unbearable. Runners were practically stacked on top of one another, sharing blankets, sleeping bags, and big black garbage bags. I found a few strangers that had some extra room under a large blanket and forced myself in. I asked another runner if I could wear his extra pair of socks, I put on some discarded gloves and a hat that I spotted nearby, and I closed my eyes, repeating my pre-race mantra. "One day, I will not be able to do this, but today is not that day!" A sudden wind gust nearly lifted the white tarp shielding hundreds of runners from the elements before my turn came to head over to the treacherous starting line.

By the time I reached my start line corral in the middle of Hopkinton, I was already soaked to the bone, and I could barely feel my hands or feet. The ice chunks that fell from the sky soon turned to pouring rain as the gun sounded to start my wave.

By mile three, I was frozen.

By mile five, I started to shake.

By mile eight, I could barely breathe.

By mile ten, I barely made it into the med tent before I collapsed.

That day would have been my sixth consecutive Boston Marathon finish.

For me, this is the epitome of failure. No matter what the circumstance, it is equivalent to throwing in the towel. It represents a closed mindset, weakness, and disappointment. If you have ever experienced a painful injury, had to take a job that you hate, failed a test, or missed a deadline, you know how it feels. It sucks! It seems all you can hear is the reverberation of doors slamming in your face, forced formalities, and opportunities passing you by. Your inner assistant starts repeating to you that you are not enough, you are undeserving, and you are worthless. You failed!

If this sounds familiar, do not fret, for you have just unleashed yet another powerful tool to grow Split-Second Courage. This is all a part of your evolution in eliciting more courageous decisions after encountering seemingly debilitating roadblocks.

Remember: Let yourself "feel all the feels" and go to "that dark place," but only for a little while. It's time to revisit your SSC Tools from chapter 5 and then begin a game plan that accounts for any of the shortcomings that led to this particular failure. For me, I was improperly dressed, taking strong medication for my RA, and dehydrated from not taking in enough liquids because I was too cold. My downfalls would now be my takeaways to use as valuable tools for the future.

In addition, to fully grasp the power of the DNF, I must tell the story of a remarkable human I have come to know by the name of Chadd Wright.

I remember that day in 2018. My energy was zapped, and I still had a thirty-five-minute drive home from a long night of coaching clients. Scrolling through podcasts in hopes to find something that would provide me with the motivation and company I needed to refill my "yes you can" mindset, I stumbled across a show description that boasted of a "story that would change your life...a man that defied the odds," or something along those lines. I hit play. As I listened, right then and there, I knew I had to find a way to talk to Chadd Wright. Six months later, he agreed to appear and share his story with my podcast listeners.

"Roger that, brother," will never sound as comforting and melodic as when it is spoken in a deep-voiced southern accent by a real-life superhero. Chadd Wright, a self-proclaimed Georgia country boy, didn't much care for formal schooling or organized sports, but at an early age, he made up his mind that he would be a Navy SEAL.

Like many young men, Chadd enlisted in the Navy and completed boot camp, but his eyes remained firm on serving his country as a SEAL. There was no other option. So, when the Navy told Chadd he would never be a SEAL and turned him away from continued training due to the pericardial cyst attached to his heart, it was particularly devastating. Naval officers warned Chadd that deep diving could burst the cyst, so becoming a SEAL was off the table.

But this was Chadd's only dream, and he refused to give up.

Freshly discharged from the Navy, Chadd began a new mission: finding a doctor willing to perform the risky surgery to remove the cyst from his heart. For him, though this surgery was potentially dangerous, it was also non-negotiable. Just outside Atlanta, Chadd's prayers of finding a doctor were answered. With a laser focus on SEAL training, he booked the surgery and never looked back.

Less than a year after Chadd's successful heart surgery, he appeared before those same naval officers who had previously turned him away. This time, Chadd was armed with the medical documentation to prove his heart was able to withstand the demands needed of it, and he was in top physical condition. Four months later, Chadd began the training where he would demonstrate the mental fortitude and physical strength needed to serve his country as an elite member of the Navy as a SEAL.

When I asked Chadd about why he set such a lofty goal to be a SEAL, he felt that having some naivete, whether it was due to his age or inexperience, combined with not overthinking things, was key. "Even when they said 'no,' I never lost faith in the dream," he said. In addition, he said he believed "...adversity crushed the doubt...[and] persistence and consistency allowed me to build these skills." [19]

---

19 Christine Conti and Brian Prendergast, "Chadd Wright—Retired Navy SEAL/Ultra-Endurance Athlete/Creator," February 19, 2020, in *Two Fit Crazies and a Microphone*, Episode 144, produced by TFC Productions, podcast, 1:22:59, https://www.twofit-crazies.com/the-podcast/category/Chadd+Wright.

What is truly fascinating about Chadd Wright's story is the sheer Split-Second Courage that emerged after his initial DNF. Once he was denied SEAL training, he found the determination and the courage to seek out a doctor and undergo a high-risk surgery—without even knowing whether the Navy would reinstate him. The DNF was the catalyst that allowed for him to make more courageous decisions going forward, to endure the horrific Basic Underwater Demolition/SEAL (BUD/S) training, and to be confident on covert missions. It was the driving force that led to his future success. A DNF is a powerful experience to add to that arsenal of Split-Second Courage Tools, and according to Chadd, he is now on another mission to "encourage people to stop doubting how powerful we are as human beings."

Although failing, or a DNF, does not solicit a warm and fuzzy feeling inside, if handled as a learning and motivational experience, it plays a crucial role in maturing Split-Second Courage. What is the number one reason people choose not to chase their dreams or jump on that opportunity that finally presented itself? You know the answer. It is the same reason you did not ask that hot guy or girl out in high school, or audition for that role in the school play, or try out for that sports team, or run for class president. You were deathly afraid of rejection, of failure, of humiliation, and of how you would handle it. Beginning even before you made that conscious decision to "do something or do nothing," Mr. Frontal Lobe, that part that sits at the front of your brain, provided you with a clear but frightening projection of your future.

While acting as your personal consultant, it would be nice if the frontal lobe provided an unbiased, objective opinion about the effect of your decisions, but instead, it flashes to the most unsettling effects of failing. You are turned down by that hottie, rejected for the role in the play, cut from the team, and you lose the election. You never get another date, everyone talks about you behind your back, you sit by yourself at lunch and must pretend you are not texting your mom, and you will most likely be a forty-year-old virgin. Do not laugh. This is what our impact bias does to us.

While everyone has experienced a DNF moment at some point in life, not everyone views it as an opportunity to grow. Now it's your chance to transform those moments into pure fuel for success. What did that failure feel like? How were you able to move past it? What coping methods worked best for you? Did you ever reflect on the courage it took for you to try?

Failing is one of people's greatest fears. This fear keeps them from chasing dreams and making uncomfortable decisions. Therefore, the more experience you have in dealing with failure, the more courage you will have to try something new. The understanding that you will not always win and the ability to appropriately react if you don't finish will lead not only to greater success but also a greater sense of fulfillment.

In fact, when your mind is beginning to turn to the "dark side," that's the signal to start implementing the Split-Second Courage Tools you have learned to handle any obstacle before you. Remember those skills you learned in chapter 7? Use them! Your failure doesn't have to bring you to your knees. It means you now have the knowledge to handle any worst-case scenario. In fact, you will be able to make more courageous decisions when you understand the power of accepting a possible DNF!

On a side note, when I was in eleventh grade, the basketball coach approached me to play on the varsity team because of my height. I was already an athlete in three varsity sports, and he assumed that my athletic ability would easily translate to the basketball court. While I enjoyed watching the sport and spent many nights as a kid playing OUT with my dad in the backyard, I knew nothing about actual basketball.

I remember those seemingly endless lunch hours spent listening to the coach attempt to teach me the rules, player positioning, and even offensive and defensive plays. I really appreciated his effort and belief in me, but I was not a basketball player, and the thought of stepping on the court of a varsity team scared the hell out of me.

I will never forget that Friday night home game. I can still vividly remember that combined scent of floor wax and sweat. The bleachers were surprisingly packed for a girls' basketball game, and in the crowd sat my mom and dad, a handful of teachers—including one of my favorites, Mr. Walsh—and of course, that hot guy that played basketball for some college in Rhode Island that I had plans with after the game. Coach put me in as the center. I ran up and down the court like a wild cheetah, attempting to guard various girls on the opposing team. In all honesty, it was a huge, disastrous whirlwind—that is, until I was suddenly wide open. My teammate passed me the ball. I stopped. I looked. I took a shot. I scored!

The crowd went silent. My teammates yelled at me, my coach put his hands over his eyes, and the opposing team received two points.

I had scored in the wrong basket.

Coach immediately subbed me out, and as I sat on the bench, tears welled up in my eyes. Before a packed gym, my teammates, parents, teachers, coaches, and that hot guy, I experienced one of the most embarrassing and traumatizing moments of my young athletic career. This moment is forever seared into my brain, but I must tell you, I survived.

I survived. While this was far from a life-or-death DNF, what I learned from that experience is something I keep with me in my arsenal of Split-Second Courage Tools. Before I make a decision that requires courage, could one of the outcomes result in failure or embarrassment? I have revisited the moment when I scored in the wrong basket at that packed gym hundreds of times to help me remember that, whatever happens, I have survived incredible embarrassment, and I will survive the next incredible embarrassment, too.

Your experience is one of the greatest tools in your arsenal. Now you don't have to avoid worst-case scenarios: Use them.

Remember when you failed to finish that project at school or at work? Remember when you failed at recreating that perfect meal you saw featured on the Food Network last week? Remember when you failed to make the team or failed your first driver's test? (I could fill a notebook with the number of times I have failed at things in life or was deemed "not good enough.") However, what did you learn? Did you move on? Did you survive? I'll bet you did!

No matter the type of DNF, if you have been through it once, you have information stored in your brain about how to handle similar situations in the future. What would you do to prevent failure, and how would you better embrace it when it happens?

Go ahead!

Fail greatly!

I dare you!

Reflection: Dare to Fail Greatly

1. Name three instances where you experienced losing—however small—since you got up this morning.
2. Name three instances where you experienced losing as a child.
3. Name three emotions you experienced after losing.
4. Name three lessons you learned from losing.
5. Name three things that you want to do but are afraid to try because you fear losing.
6. What would be the worst- and best-case scenarios of doing the aforementioned things? Now erase or cross out what you wrote about the worst-case scenario.
7. What is something that you started in life but never finished?
8. Are you afraid of failure? What does failure mean to you?
9. Name three instances in your life when you showed resilience after experiencing failure.
10. What did you change about your mindset and behaviors afterward that allowed you to FAIL GREATLY?

CHAPTER 10

Compete

"Whether you believe you can do a thing or not, you are right."
—HENRY FORD

A Daily Cup of bELieve

ARE YOU GOING THROUGH THE MOTIONS EACH DAY, or do you push yourself and compete? Do you get up in the morning and say to yourself, "today, I have to ___________," or do you say, "Today, I GET to _______________"? Do you consider each day a new adventure? Do you attack each day, or are you happy with the mundane routine? These are some of the tough questions you must ask yourself if you are serious about growing Split-Second Courage.

Competition usually means striving to gain or win something by defeating or establishing superiority over others who are working toward the same goal. However, when you decide to start "competing" with yourself, that is when real winning occurs. If you are open to learning how to make more courageous decisions and dare greatly, then you must remember that you are your biggest competition. You are the one who sets the rules, picks the team, decides on practices, and creates the life that you deserve. No one else can control these aspects of your life but you. It's time to compete.

To help you better understand this idea, I must refer to one of the most extraordinary people I have had the honor of interviewing on my podcast in 2021. He has every reason not to get up every morning and compete, but that is not in his nature. Competing is in his blood, and nothing will stop him.

It was a beautiful mid-October day in 2010 when an extremely competitive Eric LeGrand took the field at MetLife Stadium for the Scarlet Knights. He was a fierce athlete with a bright future and a winning mindset. However, little did #52 know that a fourth-quarter play would not only end his football career but also present him with a life-altering spinal cord injury.

In a split second, everything changed.

Eric, a once-dauntless competitor, lay motionless on the field with devastating injuries to his C3 and C4 vertebrae. The injury paralyzed his powerful athletic body, ended his career, and stole his independence. His once-bright future seemed dark.

Or did it?

I asked Eric about what it was like to wake up in the hospital after an injury of such magnitude.

"What was going through your head? Were there moments when you wanted to give up, or were you always ready to compete when any obstacle was placed in your way?"

Without hesitation, Eric said, "Up in the hospital, I realized I had so many people around me that supported me and were reaching out to see how they could help. I 'bELieved' that I would shatter expectations for recovery and one day walk again because I always compete."[20]

Note the "EL" for his initials—that's not an accident. While Eric's slow recovery continues to this day, his competitive nature remains strong. Not long after he returned home in his motorized wheelchair, he began to harness national attention from his injury that allowed him a platform to inspire others living with and impacted by paralysis to "bELieve."

If Eric could not physically compete, he would compete using his mind. He launched Team LeGrand in September of 2013 to help raise funds for the Christopher and Dana Reeve Foundation, carrying on the legacy of the late Christopher Reeve, better known as Superman. Reeve himself suffered paralysis from an equestrian injury. Team LeGrand has raised more than a million dollars, and Eric's competitive nature craves much, much more.

Since Eric's injury, he has finished his degree from Rutgers and become an author and a sports analyst for ESPN, Sirius, and the Big Ten Network. A sought-after speaker, he won an ESPY Award in 2012 and was inducted into the WWE Hall of Fame in 2017. The Tampa Bay Buccaneers gave him a symbolic professional contract in 2012, and Eric even founded two companies. The first was a clothing brand, Shop FiftyTwo, created in 2020, where the signature product line is his "ROLL MODEL" series. This serves

---

20 Christine Conti and Brian Prendergast, "Eric LeGrand—Founder of Team LeGrand, Owner of LeGrand Coffee House," March 23, 2021, in *Two Fit Crazies and a Microphone*, Episode 214, produced by TFC Productions, podcast, 48:08, https://www.twofitcrazies.com/the-podcast/2021/3/3/eric-legrand-founder-of-team-le-grand-owner-of-legrand-coffee-house-inspirational-human-speaker-and-leader-episode-214.

to persuade those who rely on wheelchairs to compete in life each day. If that is not enough, in January 2021, Eric officially created his own coffee brand, LeGrand Coffee House. The business first launched with an online shop and a brick-and-mortar location in Eric's hometown of Woodbridge, New Jersey.[21]

He felt strongly about providing his community with a comfortable and safe environment to gather, find the inspiration to strive for greatness, and learn how to "compete" in their own lives. In Eric's words, this is where "you can find your daily cup of bELieve."

Since his injury, "Eric has shown the world that obstacles can be transformed into opportunities .... He will continue to drive his mission forward until he delivers on Christopher Reeve's dream of a world with empty wheelchairs," says the biography on his website. "To Eric, it is not a matter of if he walks again, but rather when."[22]

Empty the Dishwasher

You don't have to be a collegiate athlete, experience a major life trauma, or stay up all hours of the night working to outdo your co-workers to "compete." Instead, you can practice competitive behavior through daily mental and physical activities to improve your Split-Second Courage.

I no longer consider myself a highly competitive athlete, but I still consider myself highly competitive. Whether I am emptying the dishwasher, folding laundry, sweeping the floor, or writing

---

21 "LeGrand Coffee House," accessed September 18, 2021, https://legrandcoffeehouse.com/.

22 "About Eric LeGrand," accessed September 18, 2021, https://ericlegrand52.com/about/.

this book, I am forever competing with myself—striving to empty faster, fold more efficiently, sweep more quickly, and seamlessly churn out chapters without missing a beat.

You can do the same. You may not experience the adrenaline and excitement from winning athletic events or getting that A you worked so hard for in school, but you can consistently set yourself up to win in other facets of your life.

I am going to go out on a limb here and bet that just about everyone has some quirky competitive nature that holds some extremely valuable insight into growing their Split-Second Courage.

Have you ever taken great pride in your ability to do the following?

- ☑ Attempt a world record when putting away silverware.
- ☑ Bag groceries at lightning speed before there is a food backup.
- ☑ Fold all of the laundry before the oven timer sounds.
- ☑ Send that text message before the traffic light turns green.
- ☑ Respond to all your emails before the end of the workday.
- ☑ Get your kids up, dressed, fed, and on the bus before it pulls away.
- ☑ Scrub that bathroom, mop that floor, or detail that car until it sparkles like new.
- ☑ Run errands or head to the gym on your lunch hour and make it back in time for that meeting.

☑ See how fast you can drive through a tollbooth without your EZ Pass failing to pick up the signal.

If you can relate to any of the above, you can channel that competitive energy to win in other aspects of your life. It is much easier than you think.

Each time you set out to accomplish a small task during your day, think of it as a competition. If you just happen to snag a place in the "fast line" at the supermarket, take a moment to revel in this great choice. This choice now becomes one of your "daily wins." While this may seem insignificant to many, reprogramming the way you internalize little decisions that lead to positive results will add up. Take a few moments to revel in the fact that "you picked the right line." You will boost your mood due to the chemicals your brain releases from fully embracing a positive experience.

As you add up all the many "small wins" you achieve each day, your mindset will change. You will feel like a winner all the time. Don't laugh. I know some of these wins may seem insignificant or silly at first, but they add up over time. The more you can experience the power of small wins each day, the more confident and open you will become to try to aim for bigger wins.

With a heightened awareness of being a winner, your confidence will grow. Suddenly, asking for that raise, signing up for that 5k, booking that trip to Europe, or going back to school for that degree you always wanted may not seem as scary.

Practice is key! Consistency matters! You are building a new mindset, a new persona, a completely new way of living. Constantly looking ahead and competing with yourself to achieve the large and small goals you set for yourself is Split-Second Courage at its best. Instead of self-doubt, negative self-talk, or poor future forecasting, you will be confident in making split-second decisions. What's to worry about? You are a proven competitor and a winner.

Reflection: Compete

1. What does it mean to "compete"?
2. Each day, do you "get to do things," or do you "have to do things?" What does that say about your daily outlook?
3. Do you compete with others? Explain.
4. Do you compete with yourself? Explain.
5. What does having a "daily cup of bELieve" look like to you?
6. What are three tasks that you can do each day to "compete" with yourself? (Refer to the chapter for ideas.)
7. If you set a large goal, do you break it into small attainable goals that eventually add up to the big goal? Why or why not?
8. Write down all your small wins for a week, read them over, and think about how you feel.
9. How will being more competitive with yourself nurture Split-Second Courage?
10. Make one split-second decision today!

CHAPTER 11

Level Up

"Courage is not the absence of fear, but the triumph over it."
—NELSON MANDELA

IF YOU HAVE MADE IT THIS FAR, there is a good chance that you are serious about growing your Split-Second Courage and living a more fulfilling life. In fact, you may have even learned a few new tools to kick-start your very own Split-Second Courage journey. As you prepare to set out on this new adventure, I want to leave you with a few more things to consider, as well as some further tips for leveling up your Split-Second Courage after this book ends.

Find Your Blue Heron

As the youngest child on all sides of my family, I had the pleasure of being "that awkward kid" lost in a sea of grownups at almost every social and family gathering.

It wasn't all bad. I had the opportunity to learn ALL the curse words and inappropriate jokes by the age of ten, and I learned how to mix drinks well before my teenage years. In addition, I learned a lot about life from listening to those conversations among adults of various generations. I received a firsthand education about the hardships of wartime in America during Vietnam, the shortcomings of just about every person who has ever held a political office, the gnarly symptoms of some very serious diseases, along with the unwavering power of hope. In all honesty, there were some perks.

On one occasion, when I was feeling particularly out of place as the only ten-year-old at an adult happy hour, I overheard an interesting, wine-induced exchange between two nonchalant women. The younger of the two was visibly upset as she spoke about the recent loss of a loved one. While I would never know the details of her loss, that day, I did learn about the power of setting yourself free. This is the first time I heard the story of the Blue Heron.

I was sitting in an uncomfortable dining-room chair that had been propped next to the wall a few feet behind these women. The storyteller slowly sipped her wine and began.

> I will never forget that morning when I felt that the entire world was resting its weight upon my chest. I could barely breathe. The alarm had been beeping for the last fifteen minutes straight, but I didn't have the strength to lift my arm, open my eyes, or face another day. When I was younger, my teachers always told me that life was a marathon that consisted of small wins each time you accomplished one of your goals. I wanted to quit. I just could not go on without him. It hurt in every fiber of my being. Heartbreak was like no other pain I had ever experienced. I remember eventually mustering up enough strength to hit the alarm clock while simultaneously

knocking over "those pills" that would numb the pain, at least for a little while.

That was when I saw it. Something was moving on the second-story balcony just outside the sliding glass doors. The faded wooden balcony faced a southerly direction towards the glimmering blue waters of the Great South Bay of Long Island. It was midday, and the sun was well up in the sky, but this was not the dancing of sunbeams or the waving of branches from a nonexistent breeze. Something was out there.

For a few moments, I forgot about my pain and grief and stealthily pulled myself to my feet. Eight slow tiptoes brought me before the thick blackout curtains that hung between me and the sliding glass doors. I counted down to three before violently swinging my arms open and throwing back those curtains like a sorcerer casting a spell.

Less than five short feet away stood a magnificent blue heron. The only thing between him and me was the transparent glass door. He stood tall, majestic, proud, and pensive as he stared at me. Never wavering, never blinking, never breaking his stare, he seemed to know me. Immediately, a feeling of calm swept over me, much like the slow movement of a soft ocean current. That was the moment I knew it was him and that I was going to be okay.

To this day, I still get goosebumps each time I think about this strange woman's story. It changed the way I decided to think about the power of opening the mind to let in symbols of hope, healing, and "winning" over obstacles and struggles in life. That night when I went home, I remember looking up information about blue herons. What did they look like? Where did they live? What did they eat? I was blown away when I stumbled upon the symbolism surrounding this majestic bird.

I came to find out that a blue heron symbolizes feelings of calm, presence, peace, uniqueness, and balance. Encountering a blue heron is said to be a signal to look inside and nurture all aspects of yourself, embrace your flaws and your individuality, and replace any feelings of shame with self-love. For, once you love your whole self and find your own inner peace, you will bring peace to others and spread healing throughout the world. In addition, the appearance of a blue heron indicates that it is time to "assert authority and to follow your unique path in life. Listen to the inner calling of your heart and not the ideas of others. There may also be a great opportunity coming your way, but you must grab it quickly when it comes."[23]

While you may or may not believe that the universe sends you signs when you need them most, my very own blue heron started visiting me shortly after my father died. Since then, he has made his presence known at some of the most trying moments of my life.

I saw that blue heron sitting on a tree branch near my parked car at the doctor's office shortly after my initial diagnosis. He perched on a river rock twenty-three hours into my hundred-mile

---

23 Shelley Shayner, "Animal Symbolism Series: Great Blue Heron." *Shelley Shayner* (blog), accessed September 19, 2021, https://shelleyshayner.com/animal-symbolism-series-great-blue-heron/.

race, sat on the bulkhead behind my childhood home while I tended to my seriously ill mother, and he never ceased to appear when I was battling some of my darkest days of depression and self-doubt.

To me, that blue heron was and still is a constant reminder to embrace fear, be scared, feel all the feels, and realize that only you can set yourself free. By allowing myself to be open to what I believe are signs from the universe, I have stayed true to my beliefs and fostered a growth mindset that would serve as a reminder that anything is possible.

Do you have a version of the blue heron? If so, what is it?

You may not believe in this kind of sign, and that's all right. But once you open your eyes and laser-focus on what you want out of life, you might be surprised to find your own sign from the universe telling you that you are headed in the right direction and that something beyond your understanding is traveling alongside you on your journey.

SSC Mastermind

As you contemplate the importance of keeping an open mind to the world around you and accepting signs from the universe, there are a few last pointers to grow Split-Second Courage. For this, I am going to call in two "ringers" whom you may have heard of, Simon Sinek and Tom Brady.

Considered one of the great contemporary thinkers and speakers, Simon Sinek has a theory. In addition to his idea that you must "find your why" in everything you do, he believes you must operate with an infinite mindset to successfully "play the game of life." For example,

1. There are no set rules!
2. There are no known players!
3. There is no defined end!
4. There is no clear winner!
5. The game never ends!

Like many powerful mindset coaches, Sinek seeks the answer to unlock each person's greatest potential and spread the importance of a growth mindset. In addition, he stresses the importance of learning how to implement an "infinite mindset" into every facet of life to break through self-constructed ceilings and live a more fulfilled life.[24] Sinek's theory is an essential tool to add to your arsenal to further grow Split-Second Courage.

Consider this:

The value in the infinite isn't about short-term rewards; it is about contributions beyond your time.

What will be your legacy?

Finite leaders want to end the game and beat the competition.

When you achieve one goal, are you satisfied, or do you immediately set new goals?

Playing the Infinite Game isn't a checklist; it is a mindset.

Do you consider your life a series of individual days with set goals, or do you see your life as something cumulative, with each day bringing you closer to a larger goal?

24 Simon Sinek, "The Lifestyle of the Infinite Mindset," February 14, 2020, *YouTube* video, https://www.youtube.com/watch?v=UY-1-9ObaLE.

Our lives are finite, but life is infinite.

> *Are you looking at the BIG picture when you make decisions that affect your happiness or your ability to feel fulfilled? You have one life. Are you ready to make more courageous split-second decisions? The time is now!*

Bring In the G.O.A.T. (Greatest of All-Time)

Whether you love him or hate him, famed football quarterback Tom Brady made an excellent point about the journey to greatness when he said, "I didn't come this far only to come this far."

Take a moment and let that sink in.

This journey is just beginning, and it doesn't end. This is it. You're about to take the first step.

By reading this book, you have invested valuable time and money into learning the tools to grow your Split-Second Courage and live the life you truly deserve. Now it is time to apply all that you have learned. Now is the time to set yourself free and create your new reality.

Grab a pen, find your favorite journal or clipboard, and sit down in that comfy chair. Let's Roll!

Read through each of these questions carefully, take a few minutes to let them sink in, and then get ready to take a deep dive into each question.

1. Tell me something you don't like about yourself.
2. Tell me what action steps you are going to take right this second to change this. No, really. Make ONE decision RIGHT NOW!

3. What does Split-Second Courage mean to you?
4. When in your life have you shown Split-Second Courage?
5. How did that make you feel? Why?
6. How did others react to this? How was it received?
7. Do you keep people in your life who hold you down or are unsupportive?
8. Why are you allowing yourself to be "tamed"?
9. What do you believe would happen if you made more courageous split-second decisions and chased your dreams?
10. How would your life change?
11. What Split-Second Courage Tools will you implement today, tomorrow, in perpetuity?
12. What does a successful and fulfilling life look and feel like to you?

You have everything you need, and time is of the essence. Make more courageous decisions and begin to feel all the feels. Embrace that which scares you. You have the Split-Second Courage to stare down fear. It has been inside you all along.

Yes, You Can!

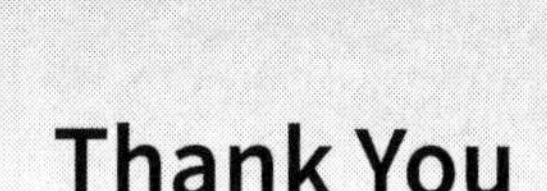

Thank You

"The most important things in life are not things."
—CHRISTINE CONTI

THERE WERE SO MANY PEOPLE INVOLVED in this crazy book project, and for that, I am incredibly grateful for all your time, patience, and support in this journey.

Mr. Walsh, as my high school English teacher, you instilled in me a love for literature and the idea that one day I would write my own book. Dad, I know you are partying up in heaven, but your decades of support and positivity are alive and well in my soul. Mom, you raised me to be a force of nature, and if anyone has Split-Second Courage, it's you! Vicki and Julie, my favorite sisters, you have always been my role models, and I will always love you!

To the entire Niche Pressworks team: Nicole, thank you for putting up with me! Melanie: best editor ever! Kim: best project manager ever! Dena: I'm playing the greatness game for you!

Brian: Your friendship is priceless! *Fit Crazies* for life! Thank you to all my friends and those courageous enough to let me share their stories: Jenny, Dr. Mindy, Heather, Bryan, Eric, Nathalie, El Correcaminos, and Matt!

A special shout out to Bryan Price for the awesome foreword, and a huge thank you to my supportive kids, Alex and Lauren, who learned to be just a little more independent while mommy was writing.

Finally, thank you to the best husband in the world! Mike Conti, you bring out the best in me! I love you!

If you loved *Split-Second Courage*, please share this book with everyone you know! I would be forever grateful for a review and to hear how it helped you grow your own Split-Second Courage! Remember, decisions take a split second, but courage takes a lifetime.

About the Author

Christine Conti, MEd
www.ChristineConti.com

CHRISTINE CONTI is an internationally accredited fitness educator, speaker, author, consultant, and CEO of Conti Fitness & Wellness, LLC. She is a former investment banker, English teacher, coach, and twenty-year veteran in the industry. Christine is the author of the Arthritis Fitness Specialist Course and co-author of the Eating Disorder Fitness Course sponsored by the MedFit Network Education Foundation, where she serves on the board and hosts the MFEF webinar series. She specializes in working with special populations and certifies instructors in her program, Let's

FACE It Together™ Facial Exercise and Rehabilitation. Christine is the co-founder of FallPROOF™ Fall Prevention and the co-host of *Two Fit Crazies and A Microphone* podcast and COO of TFC Productions, LLC. Christine is also an autoimmune disease warrior, ultra-endurance athlete, and IRONMAN. She currently resides at the New Jersey shore with her husband, Michael, and two children, Alexander (13) and Lauren Renee (9).

Join the SSC Community!

For even more Split-Second Courage Tools or the chance to work more closely with Christine, ***join the Split-Second Courage Monthly Growth private Facebook Community!*** Join Christine for monthly online workshops, community forums, Q & A sessions, networking opportunities, or find out how to work with Christine one-on-one!

Speaking Engagements and Events

Schedule a speaking engagement with Christine for your next group, company, business, school, team, medical, and/or fitness facility event. To keep up with Christine's latest news and adventures or get in touch, you can find her at:

Contact Christine

Website: ChristineConti.com
Facebook: facebook.com/christine.conti.96
Twitter: twitter.com/ContiFitness
Instagram: @get_contifit
Email: info@ContiFit.com

Made in the USA
Columbia, SC
04 May 2022

59956697R00093